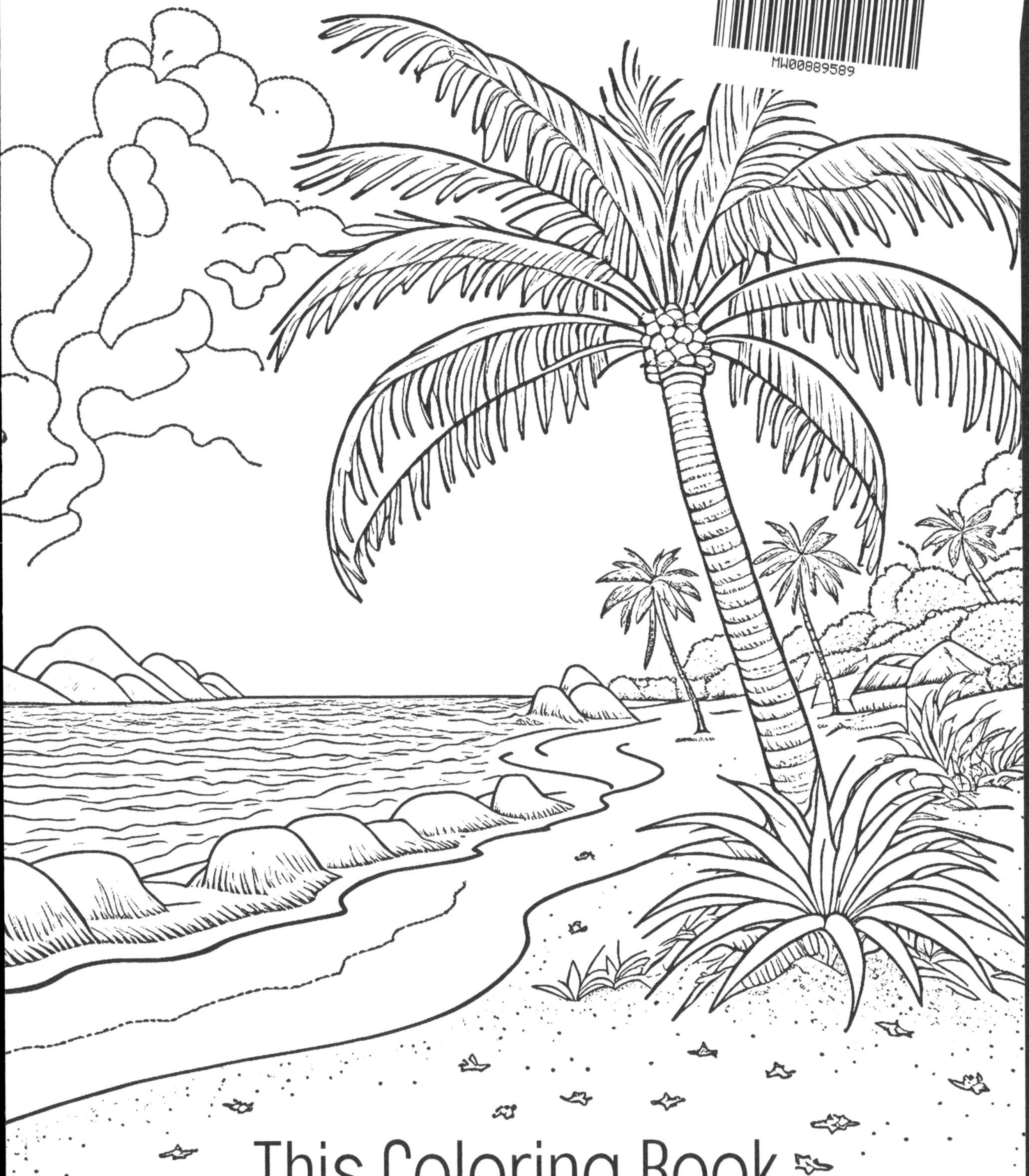

This Coloring Book
Belongs To : ...........

ISBN: 9798386477523

AUTHOR : AMIR FARAZ

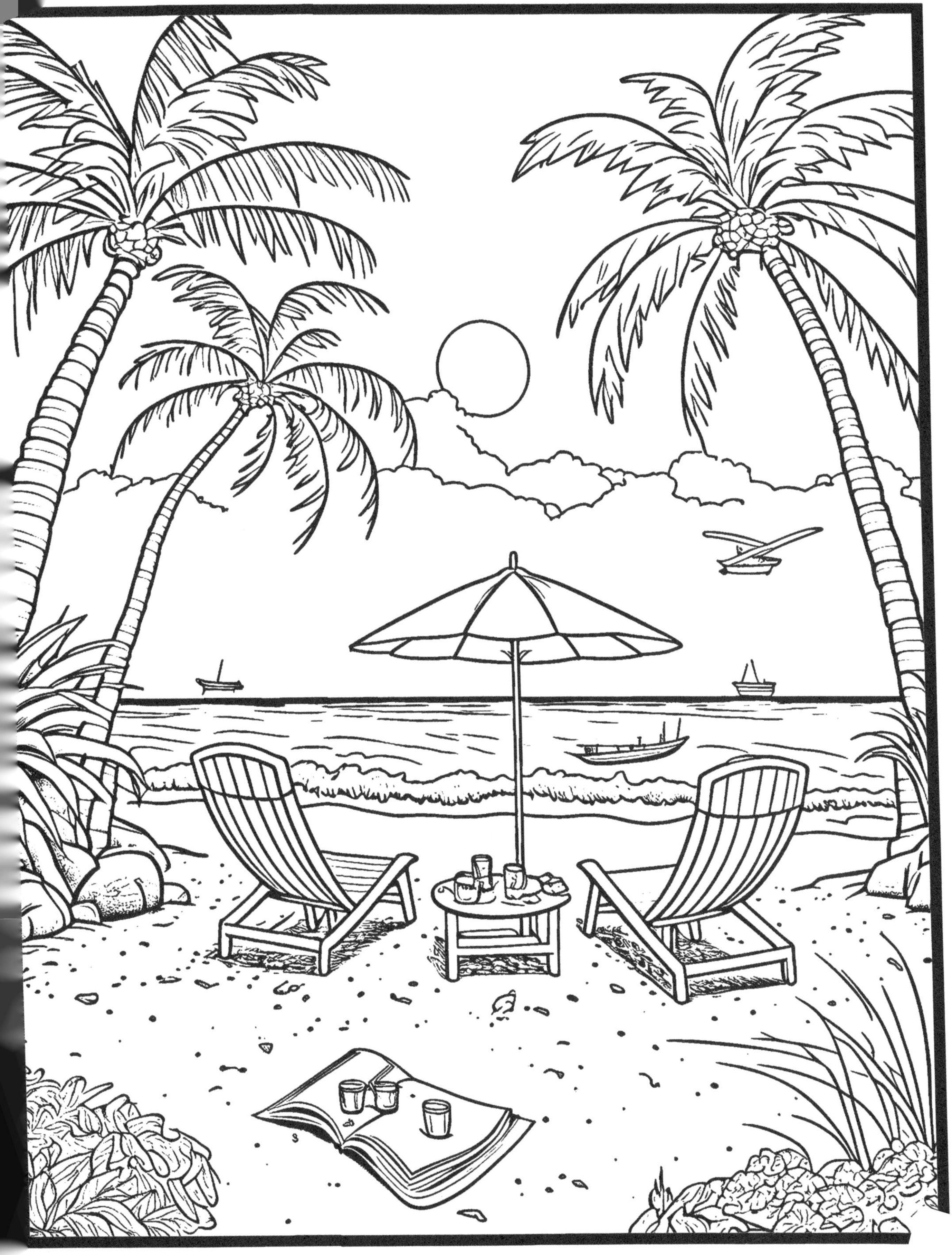

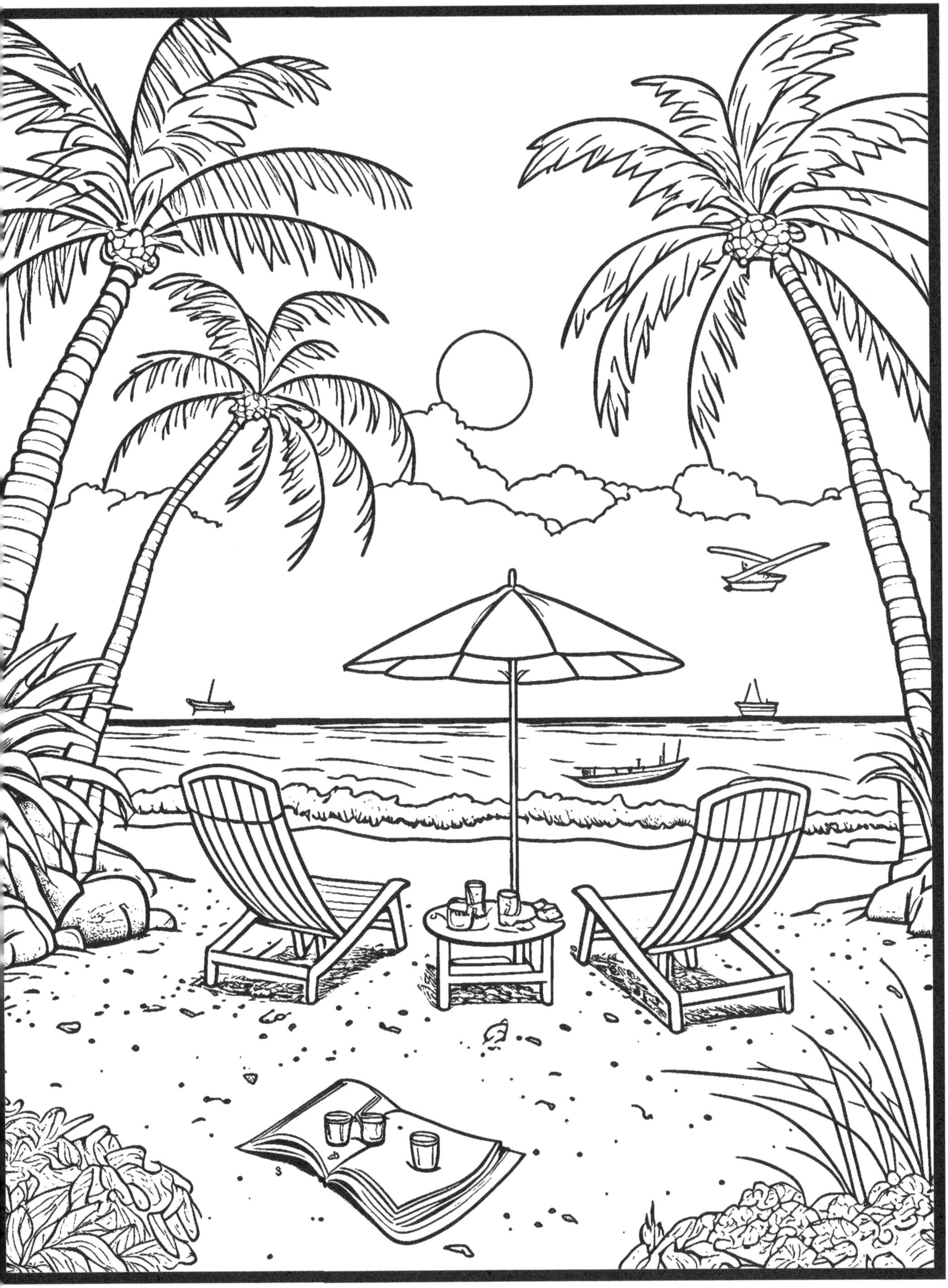

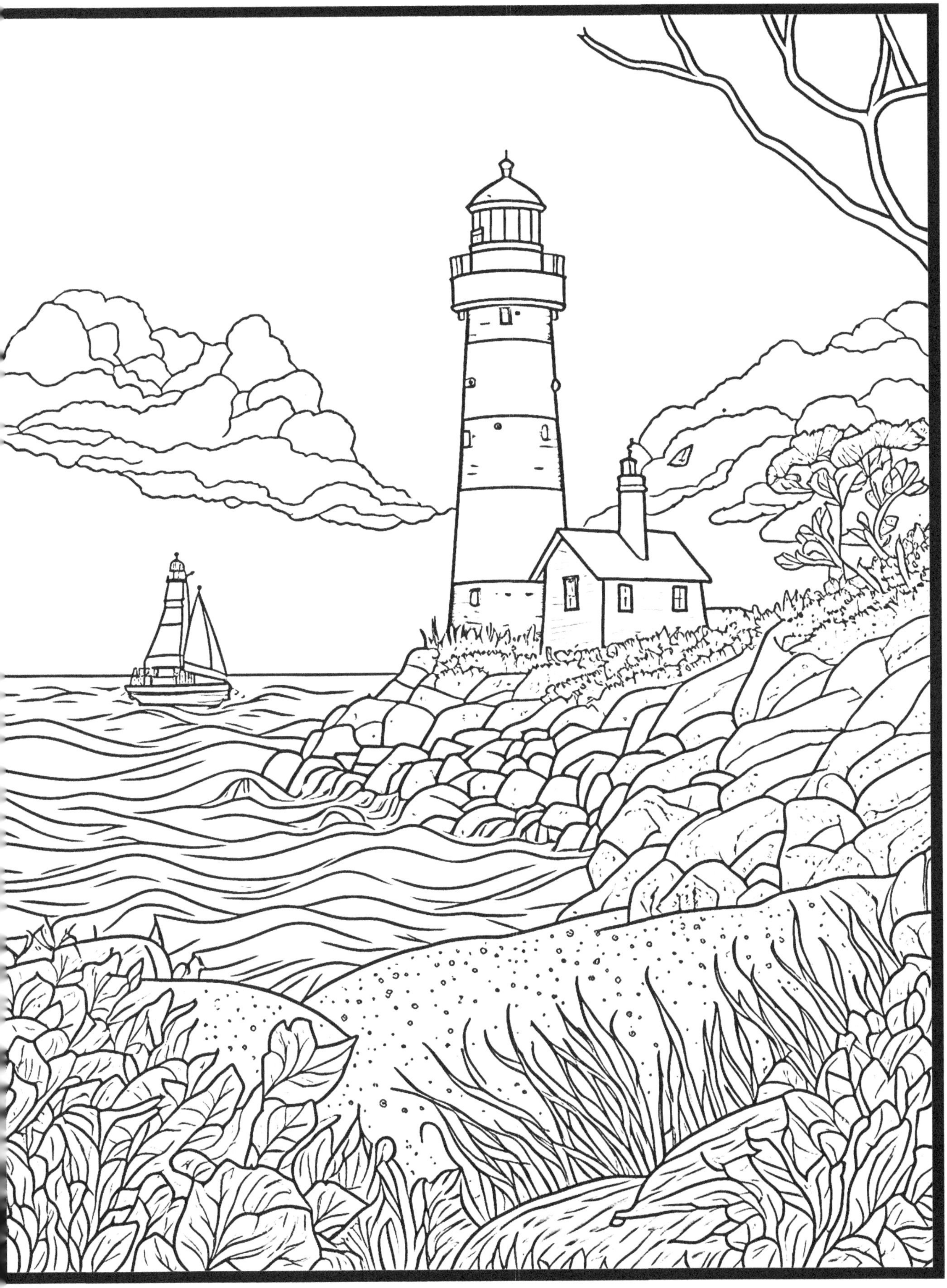

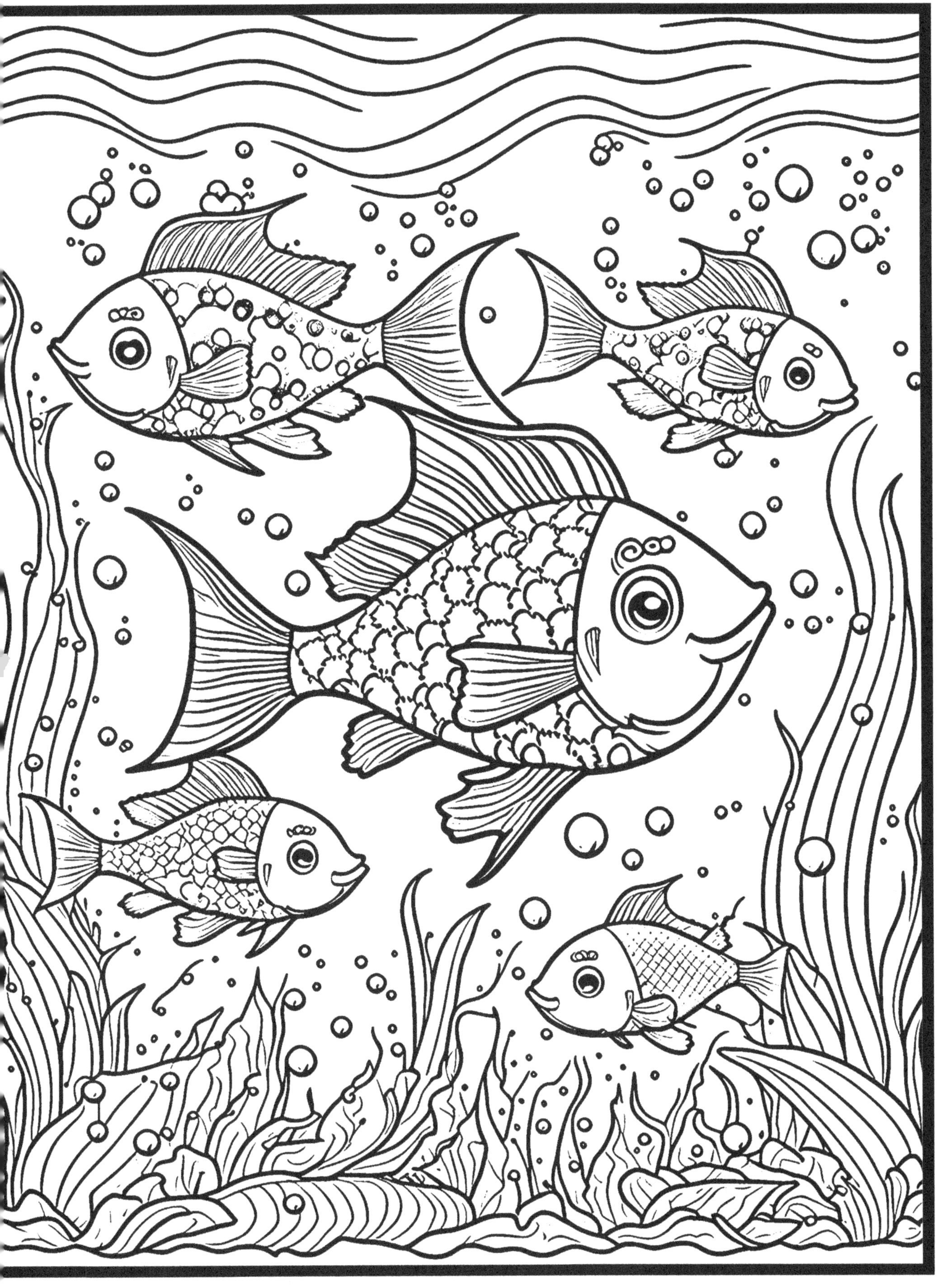

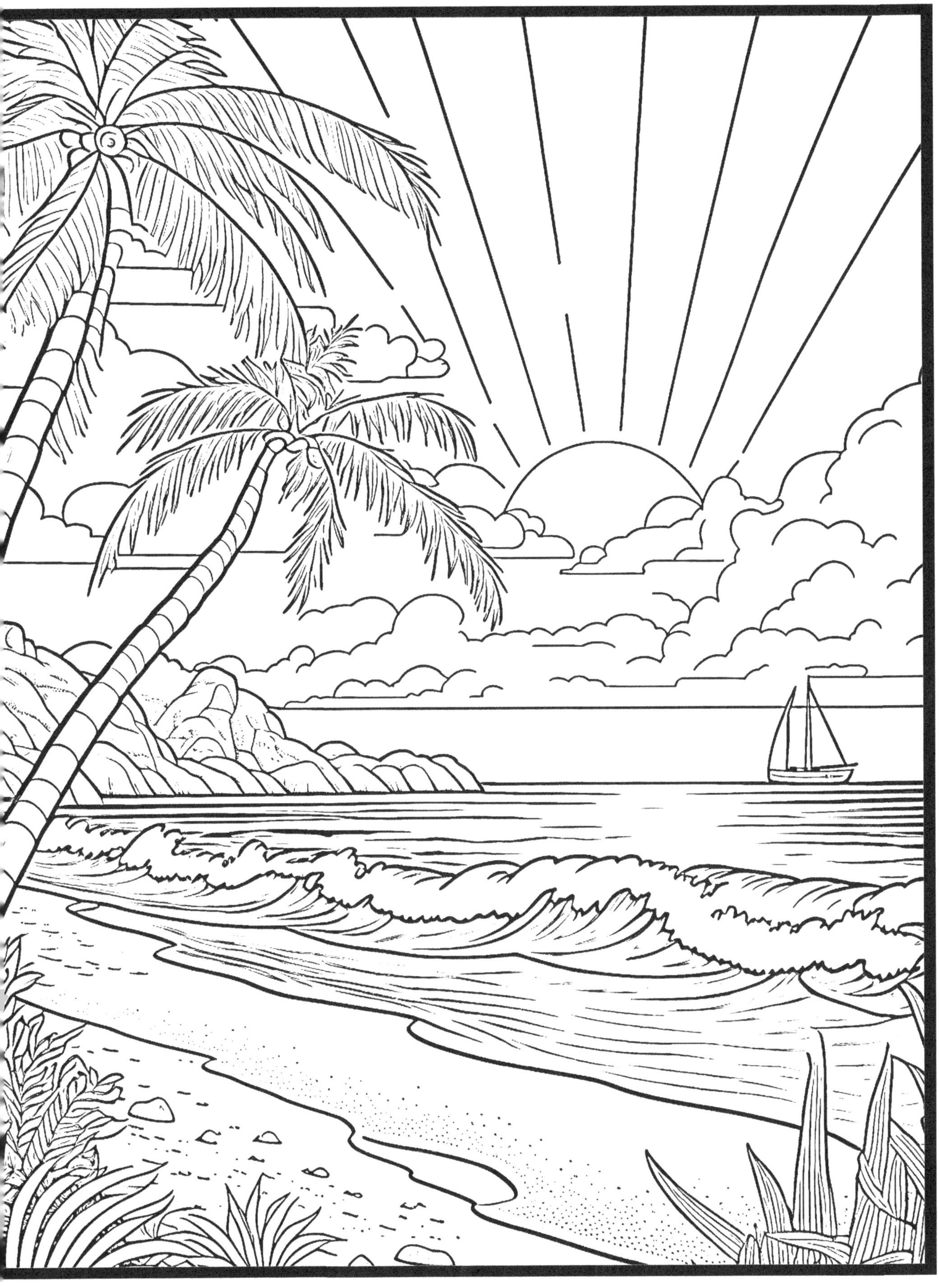

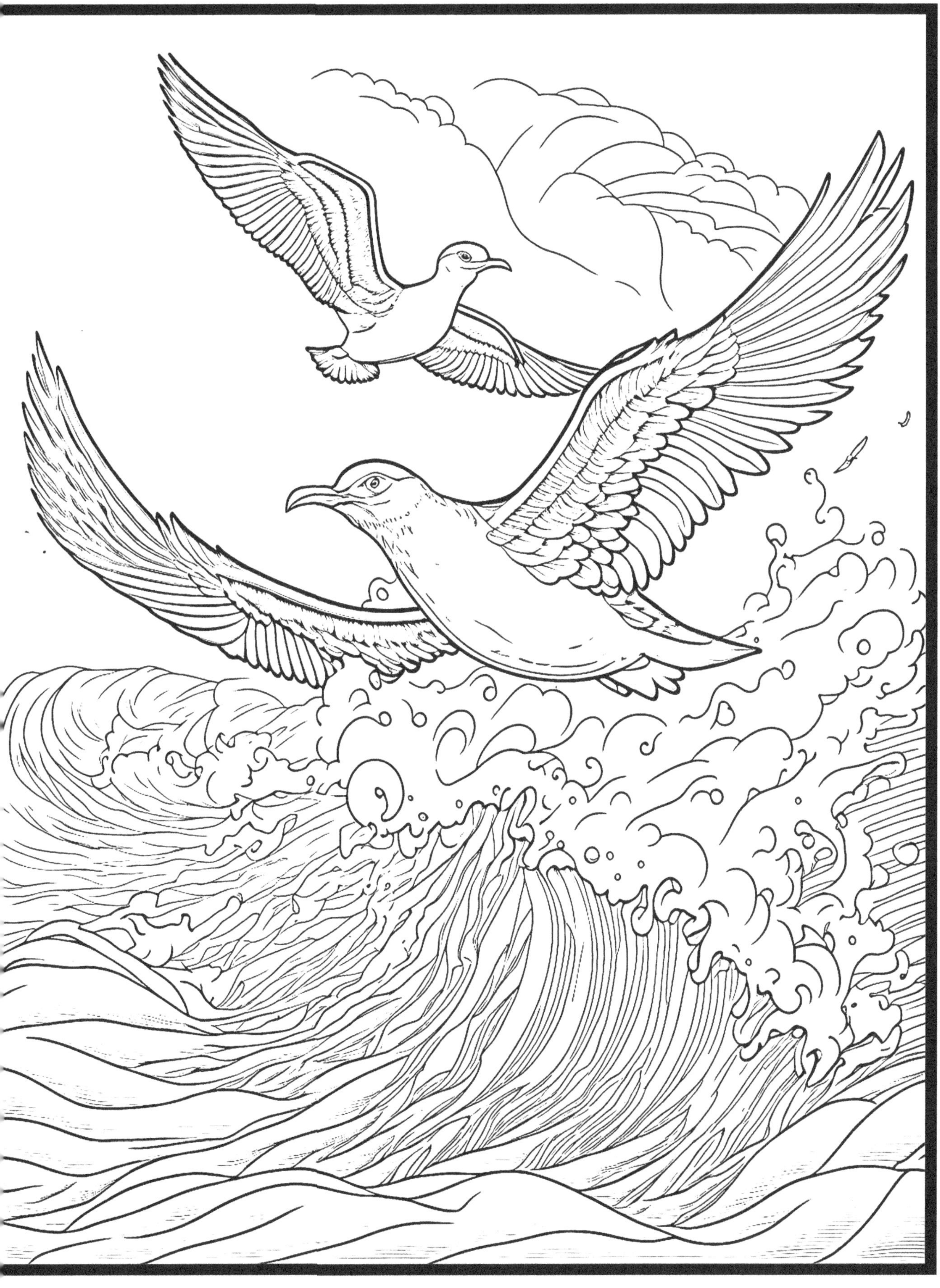

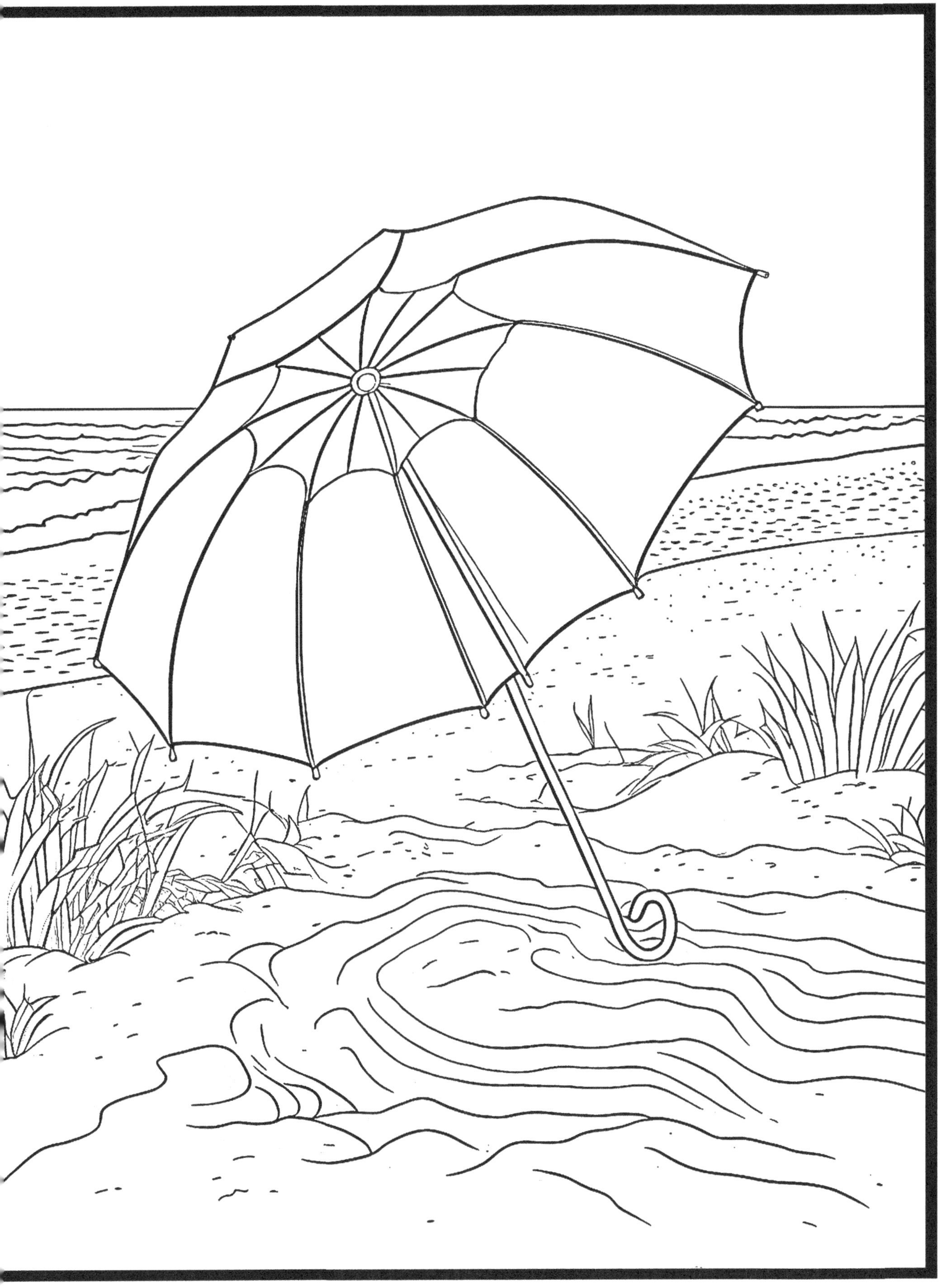

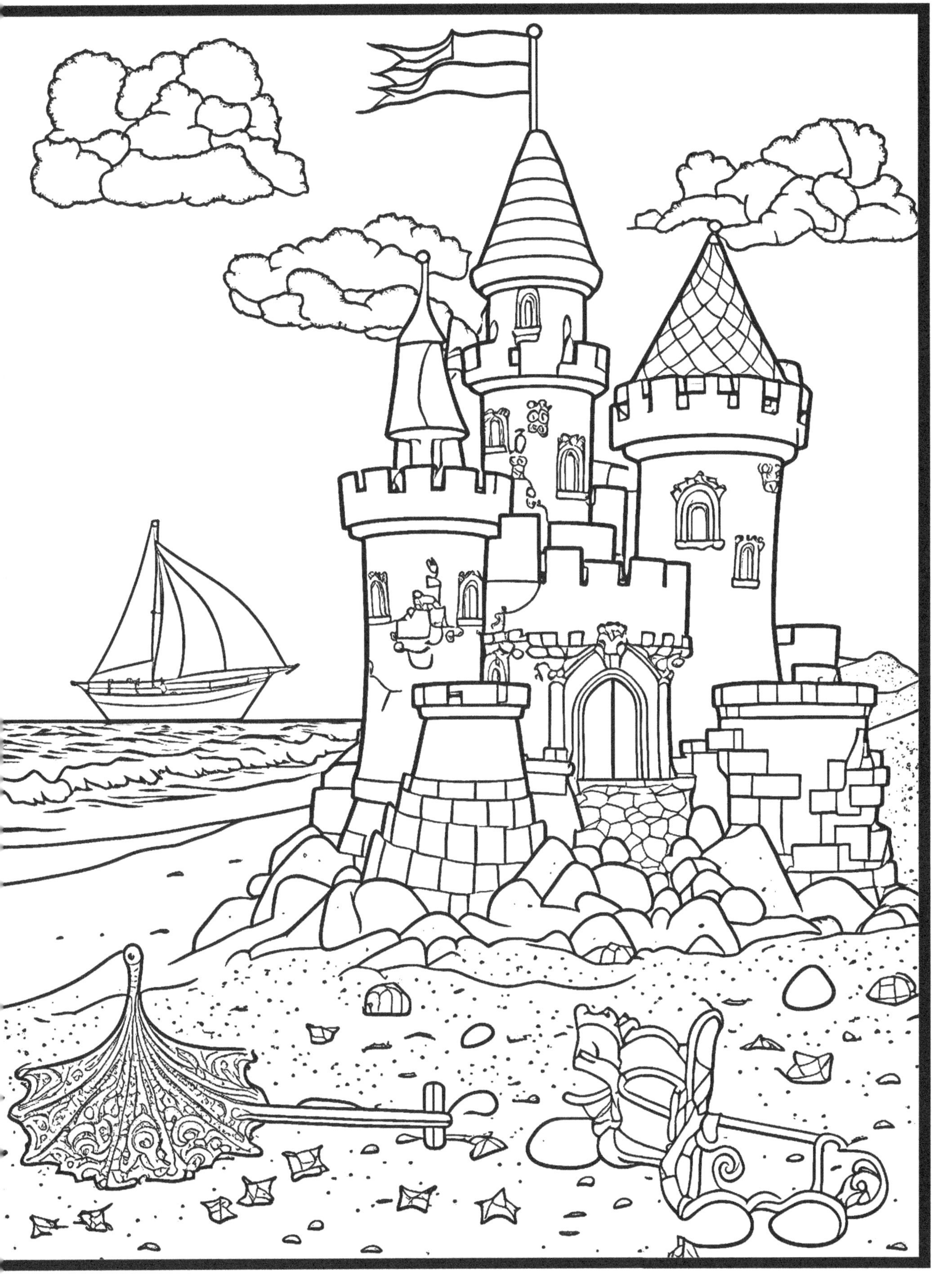

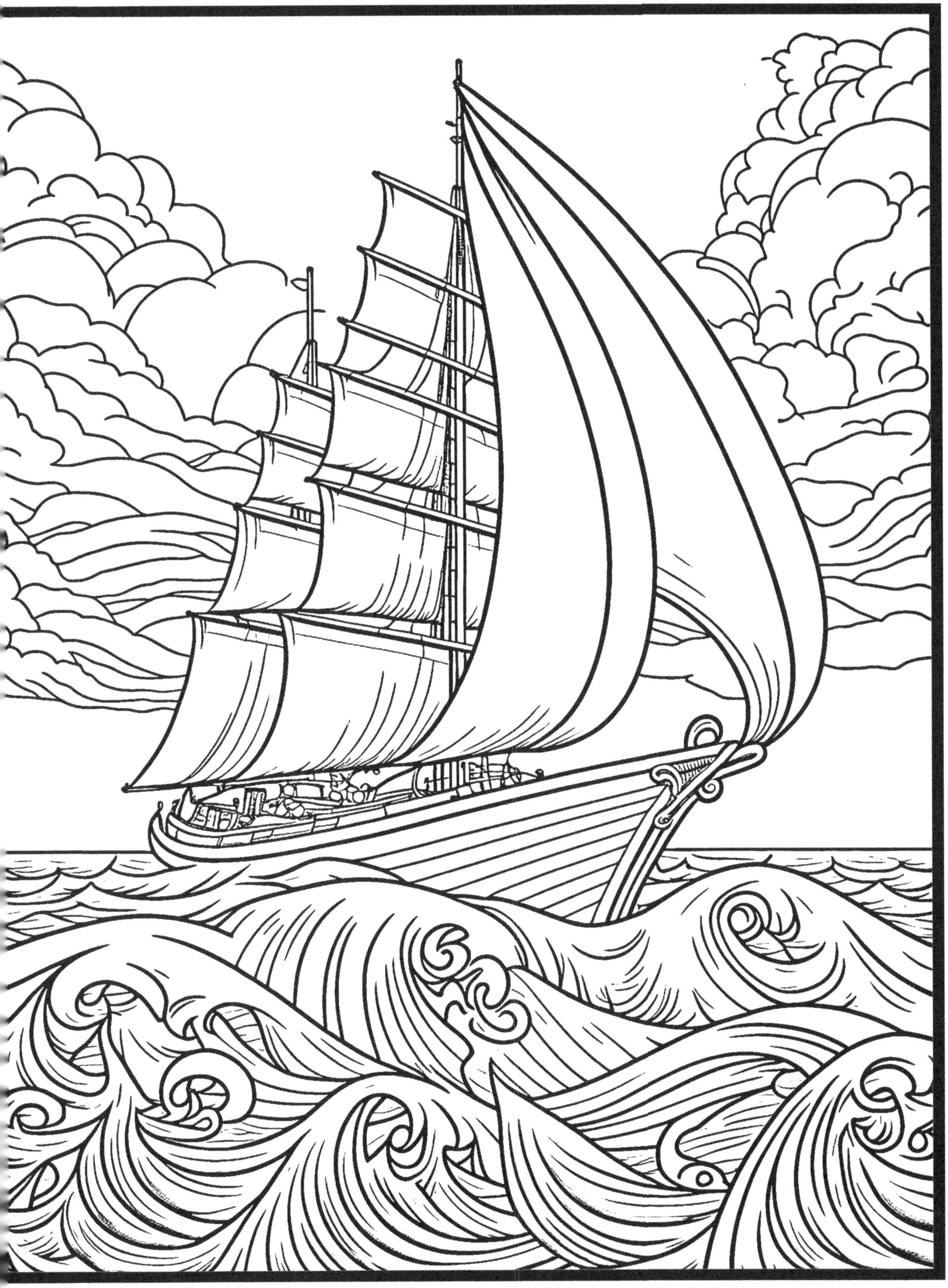

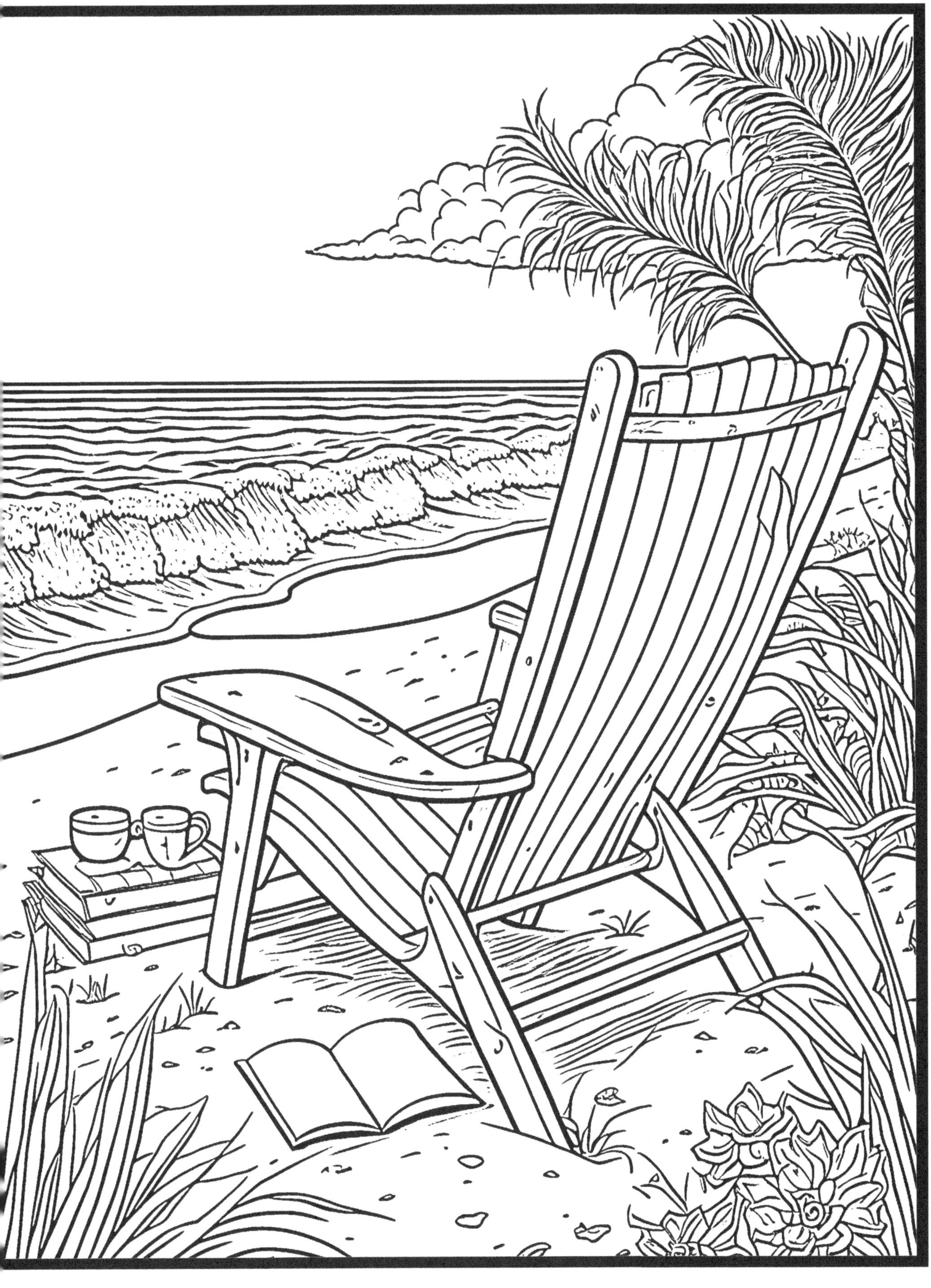

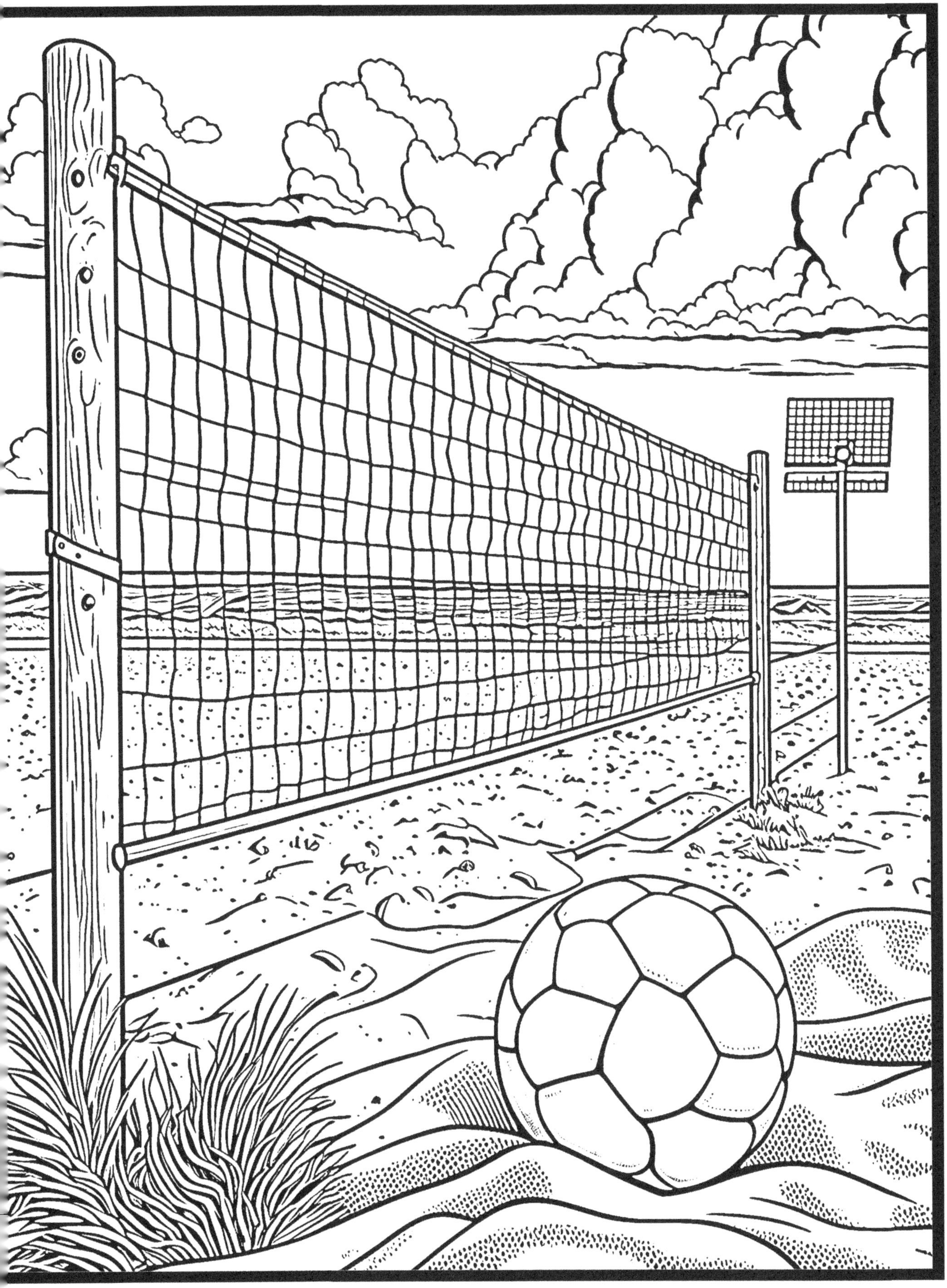

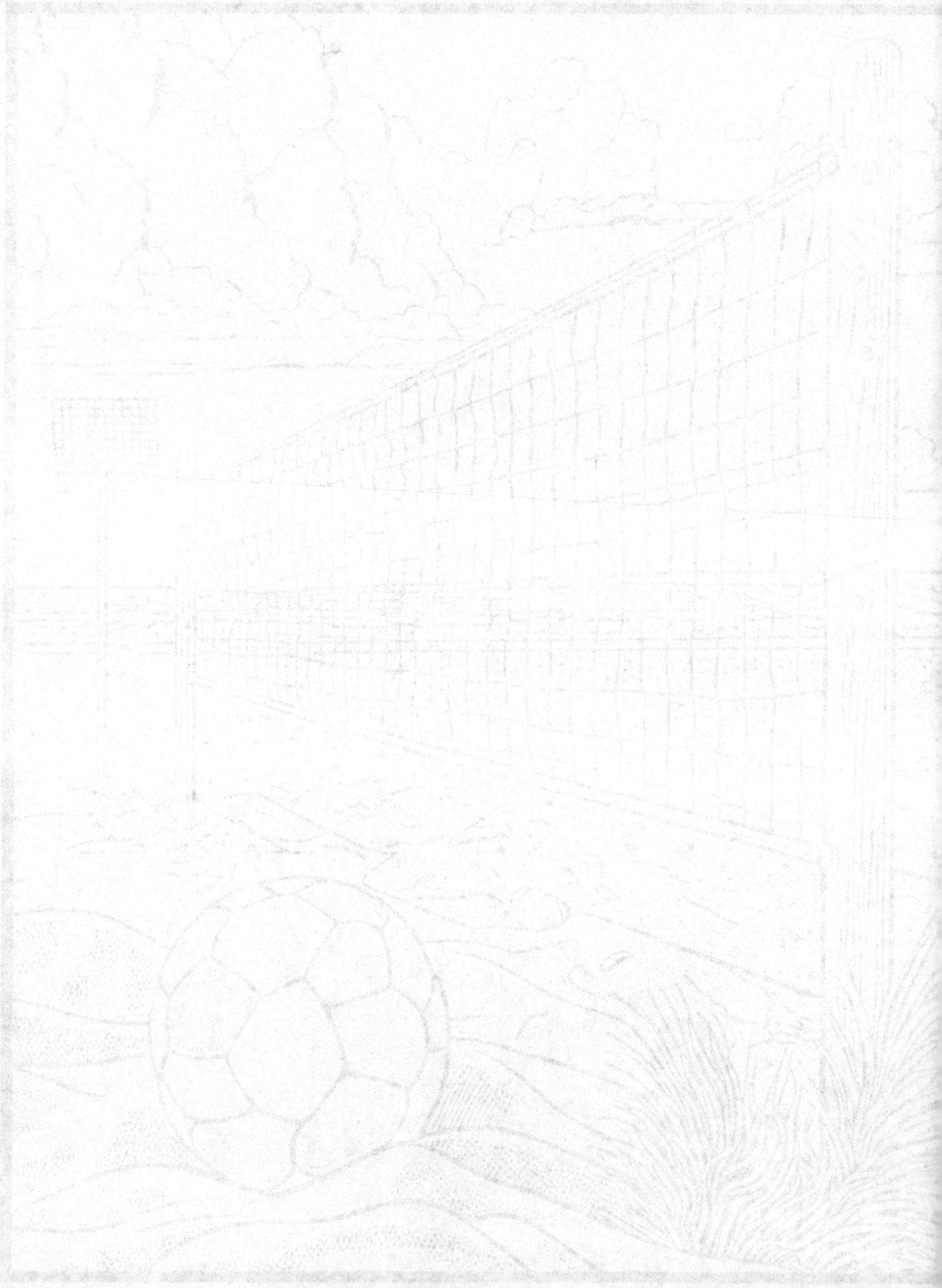

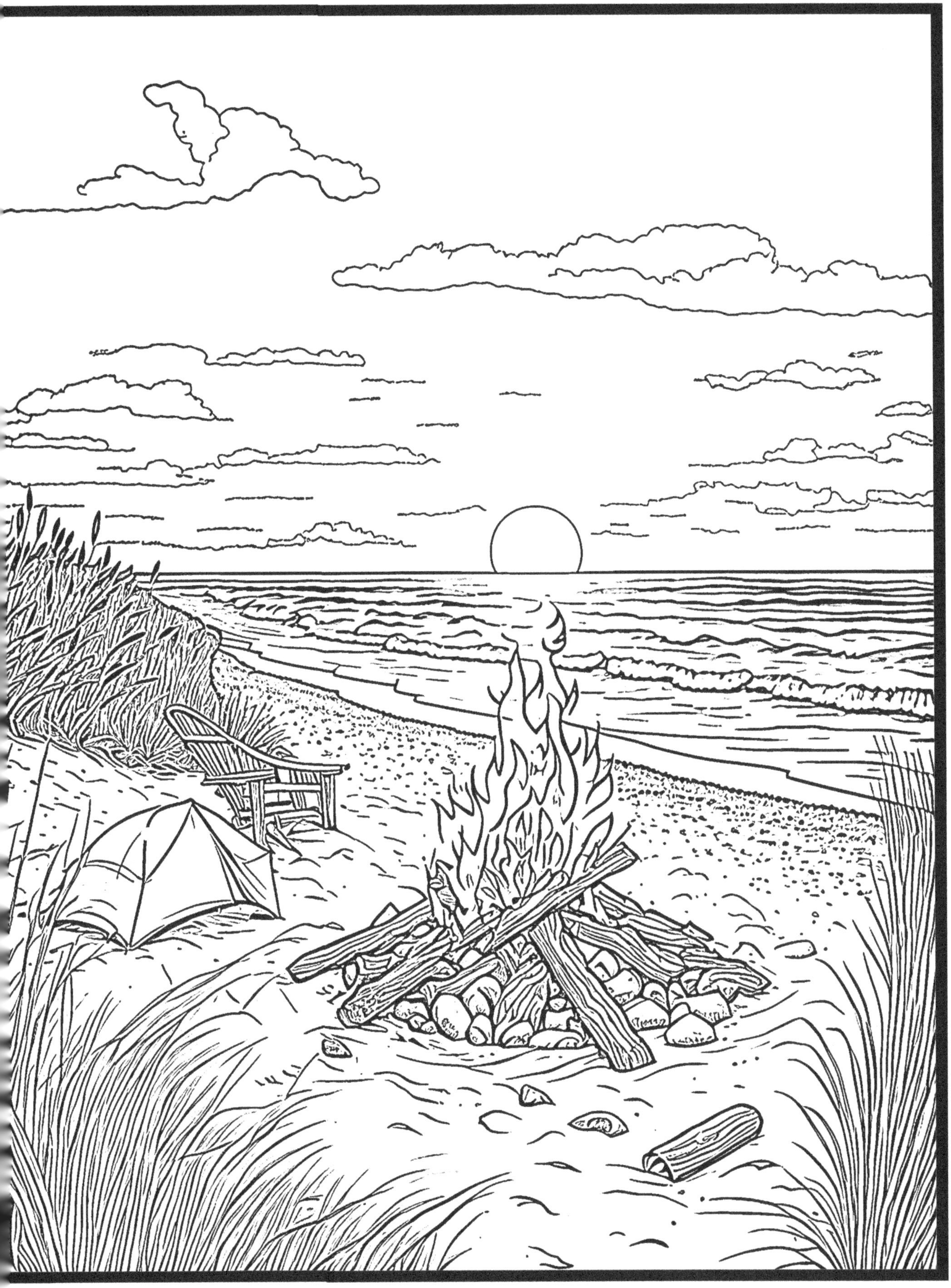

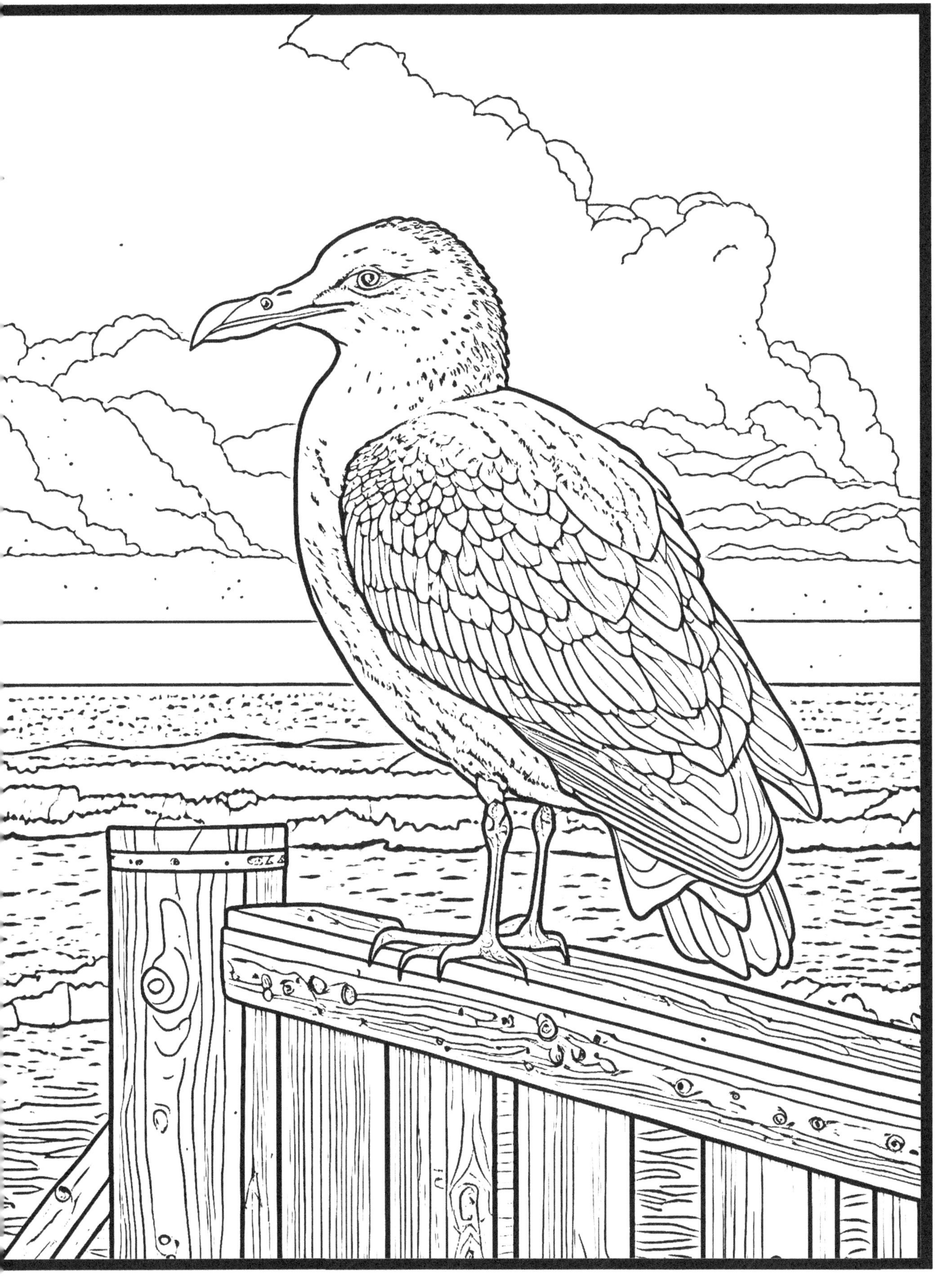

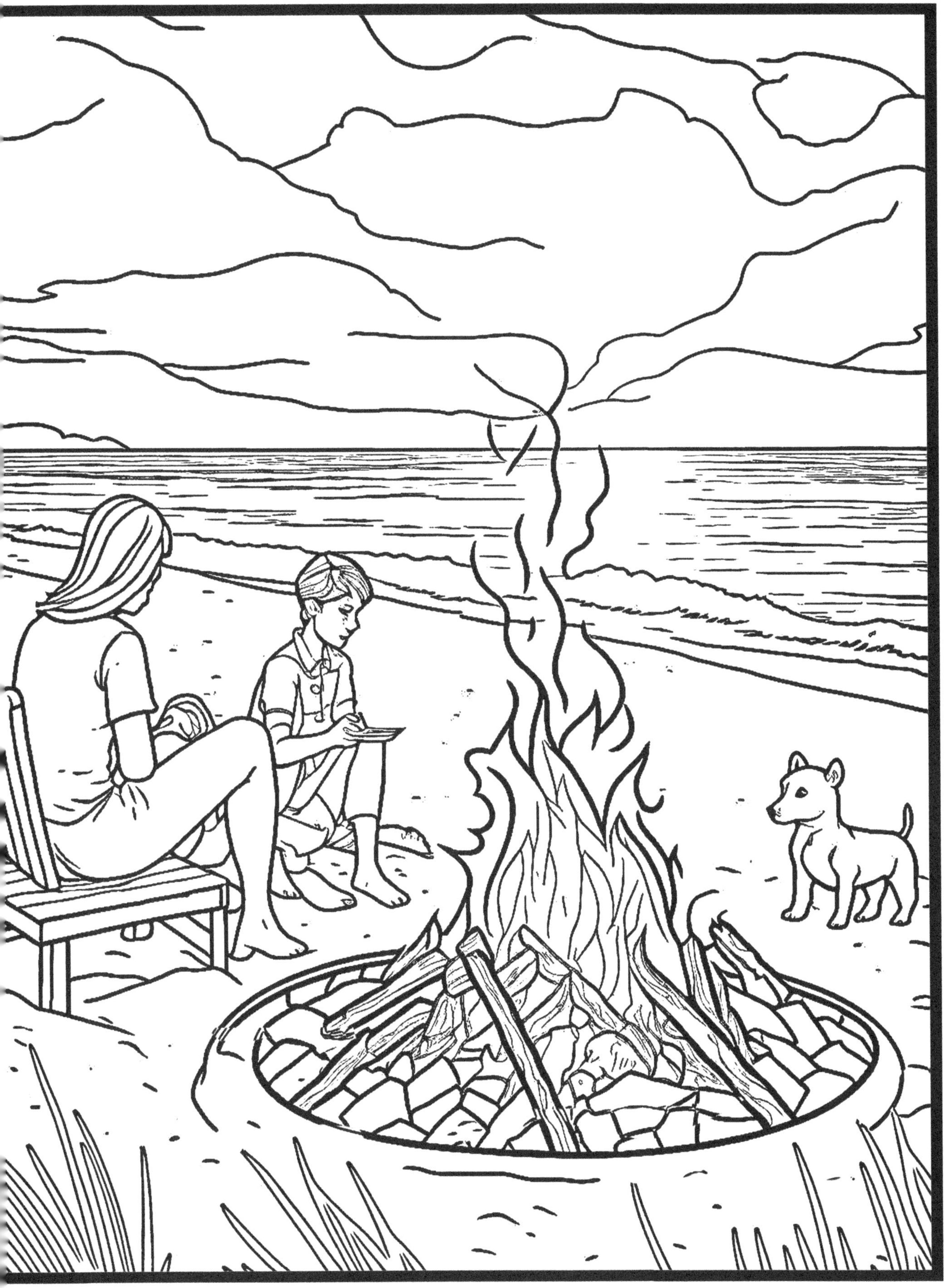

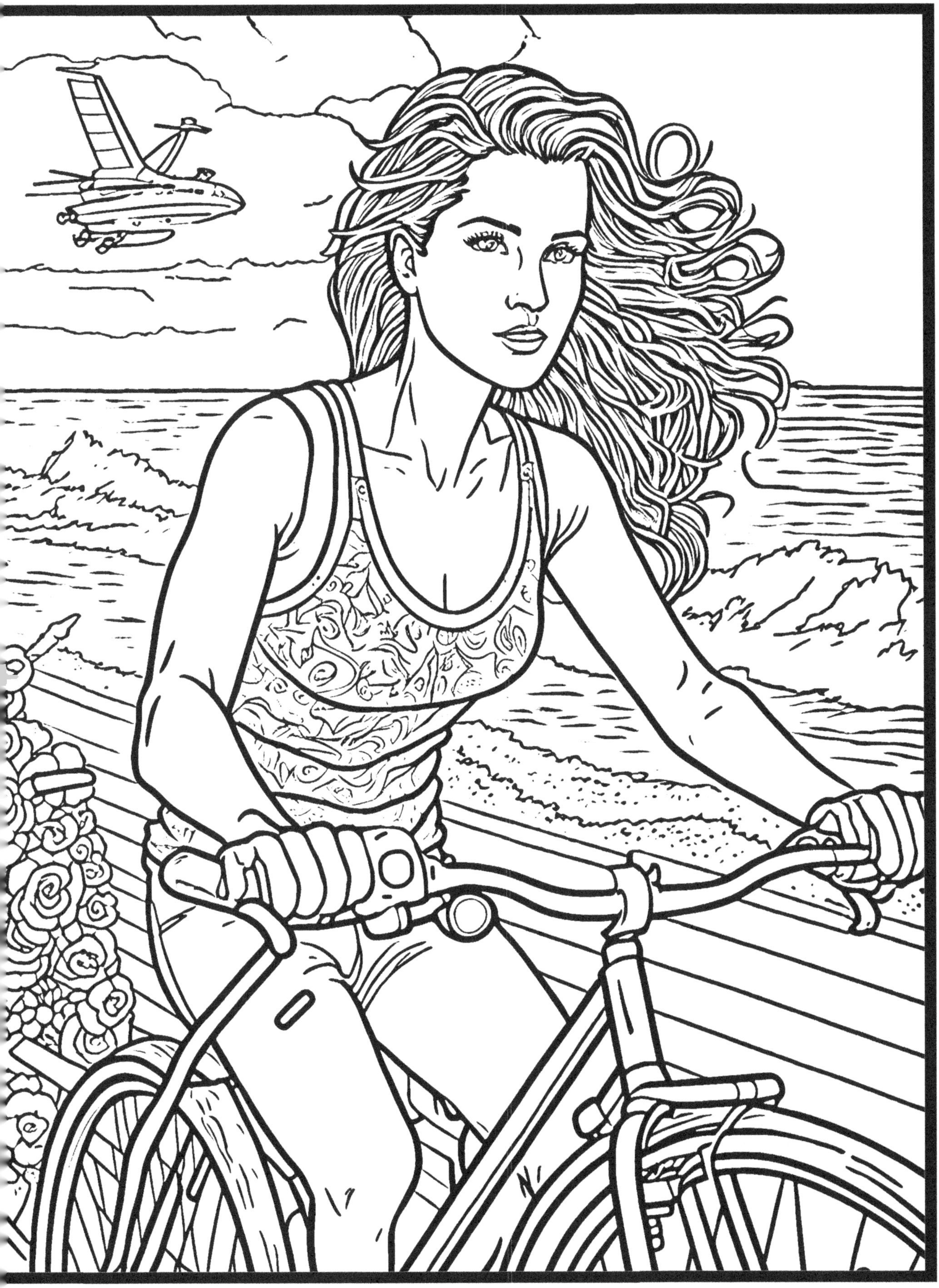

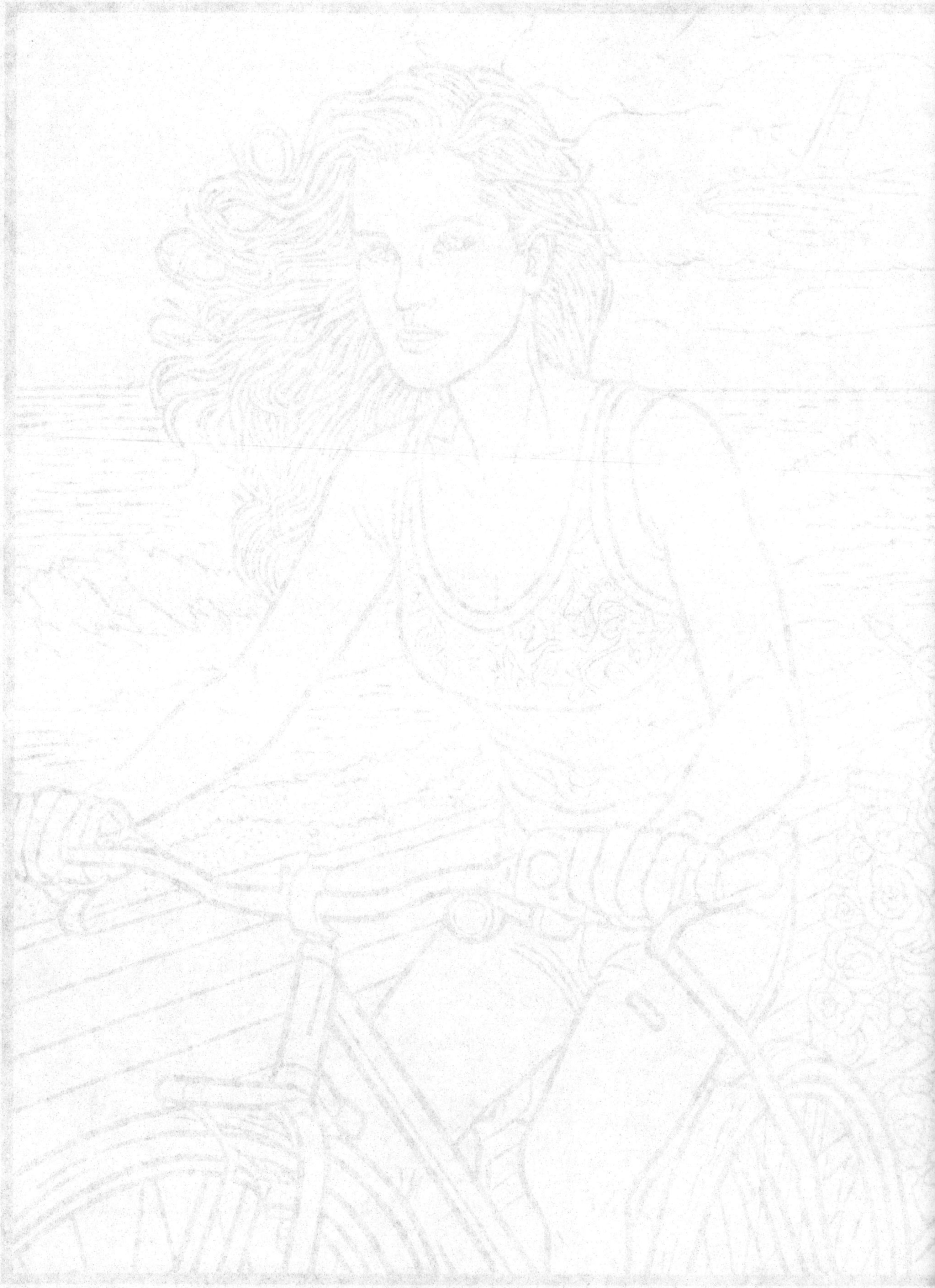

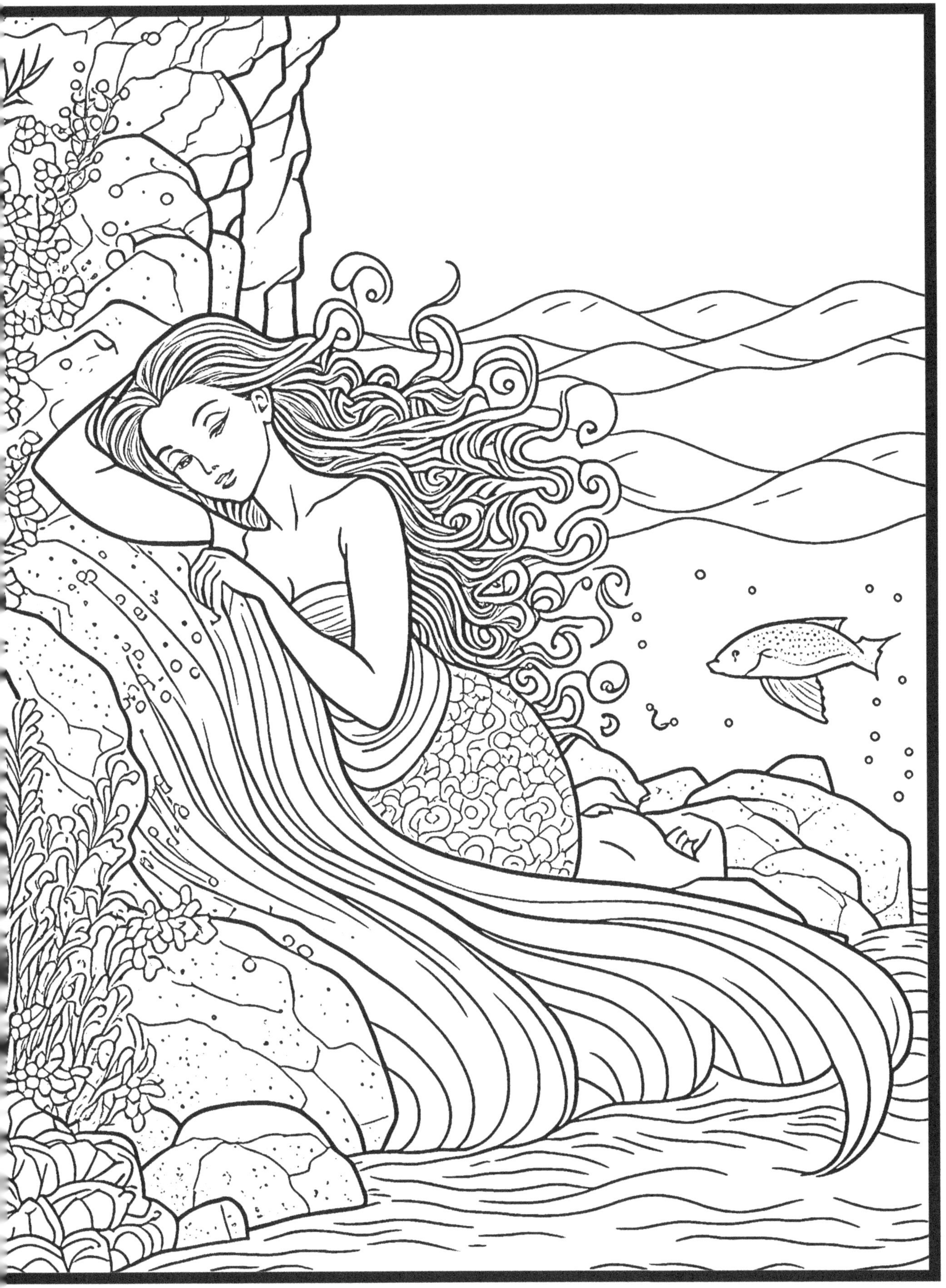

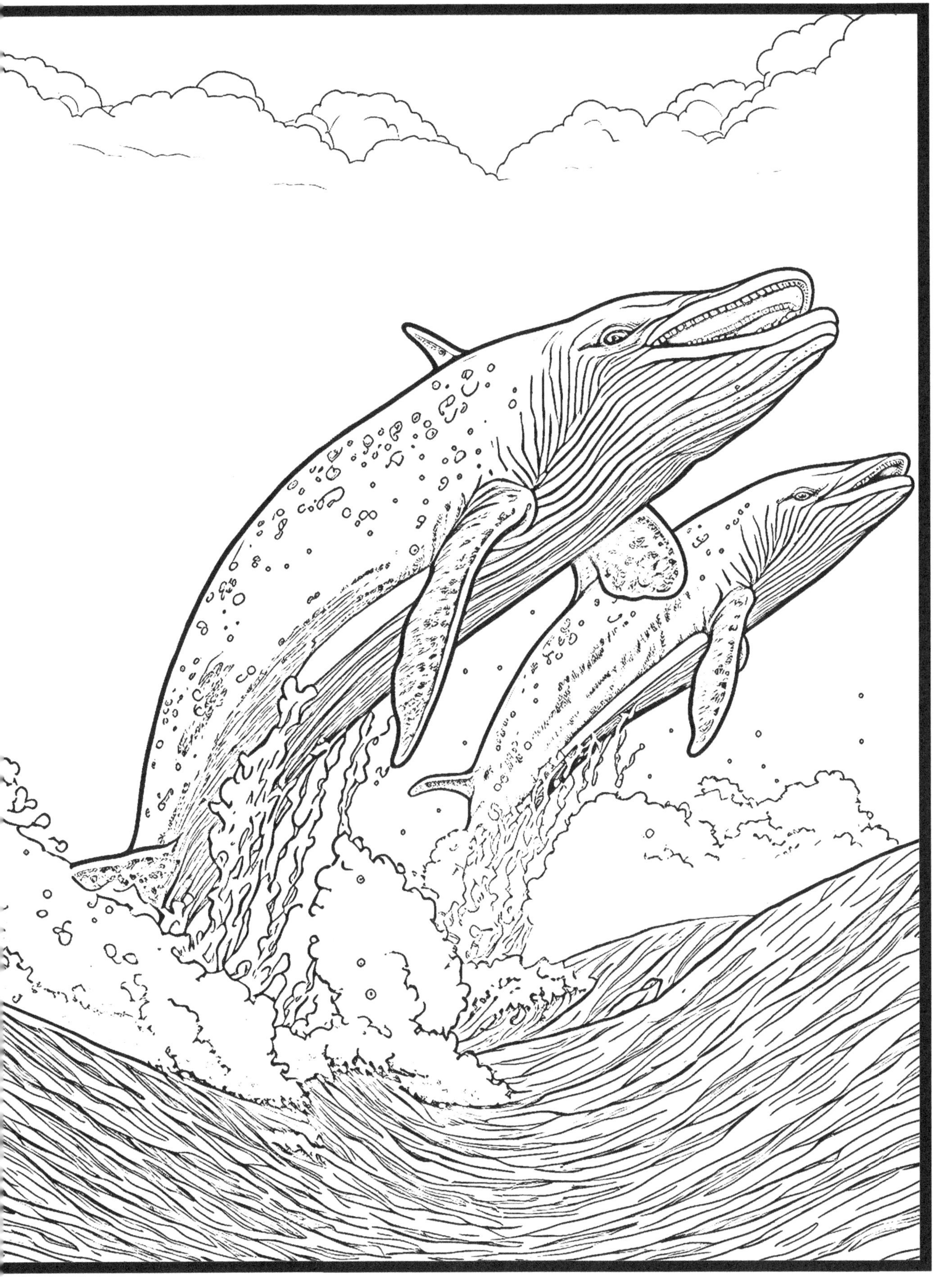

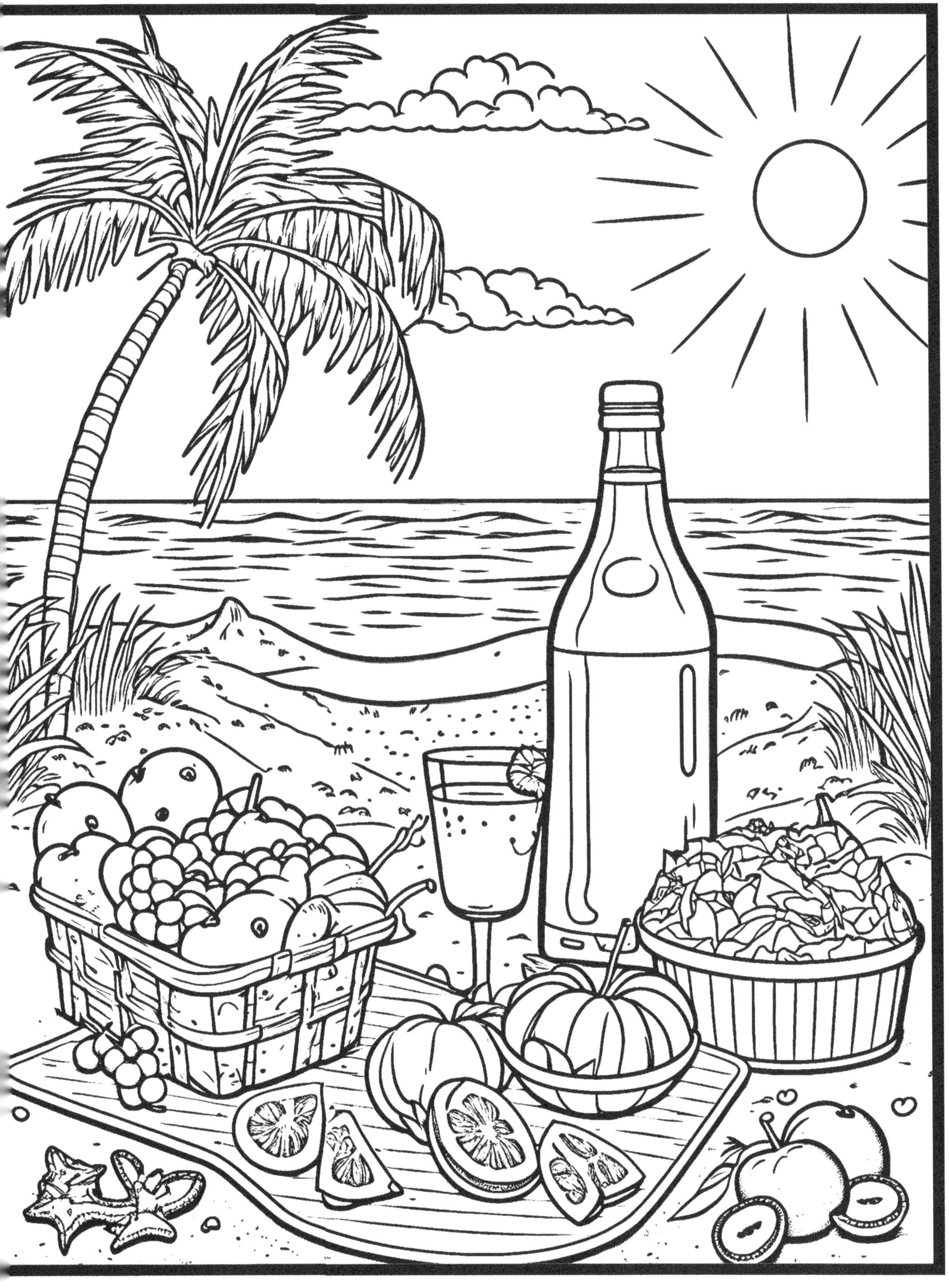

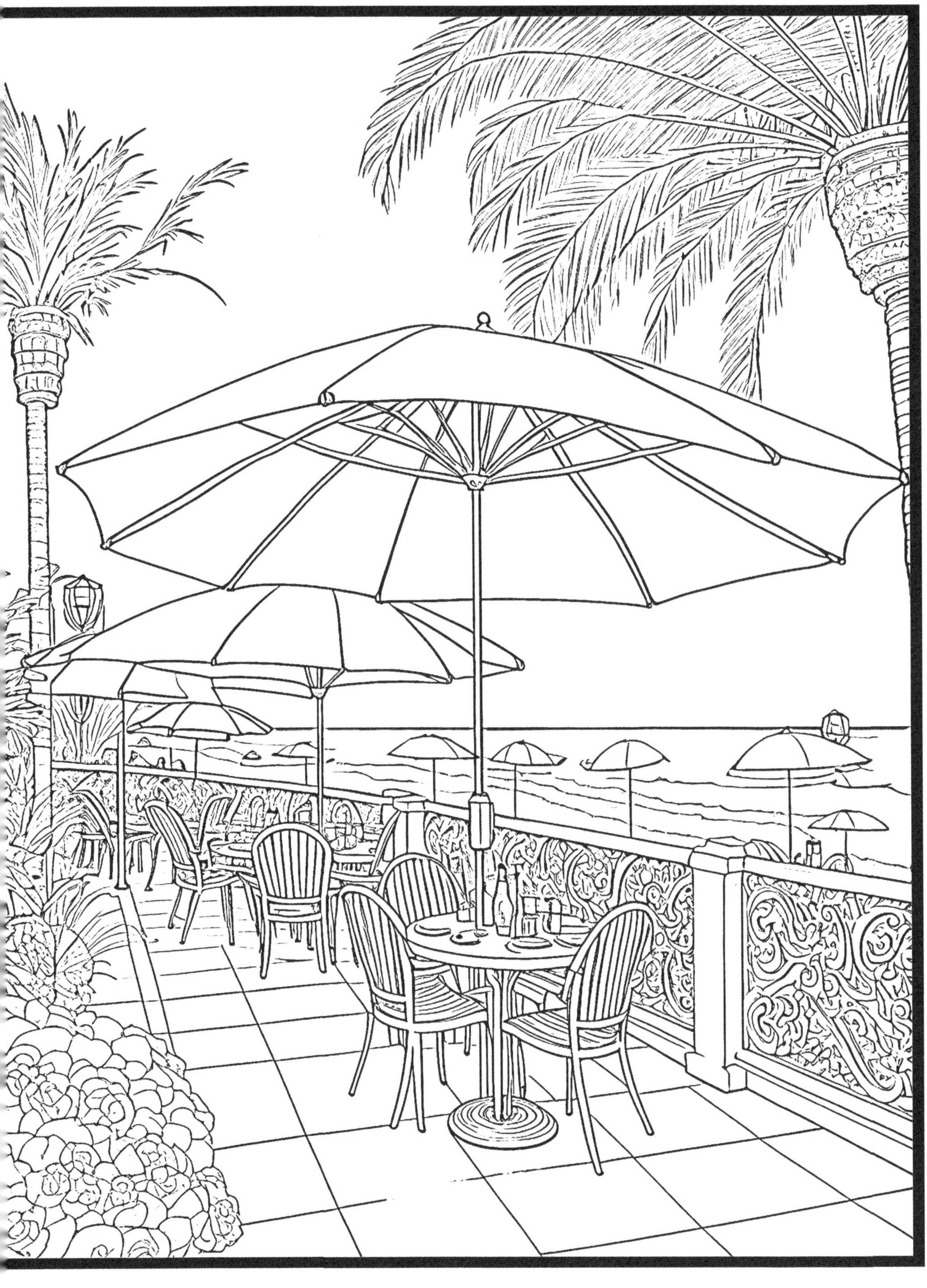

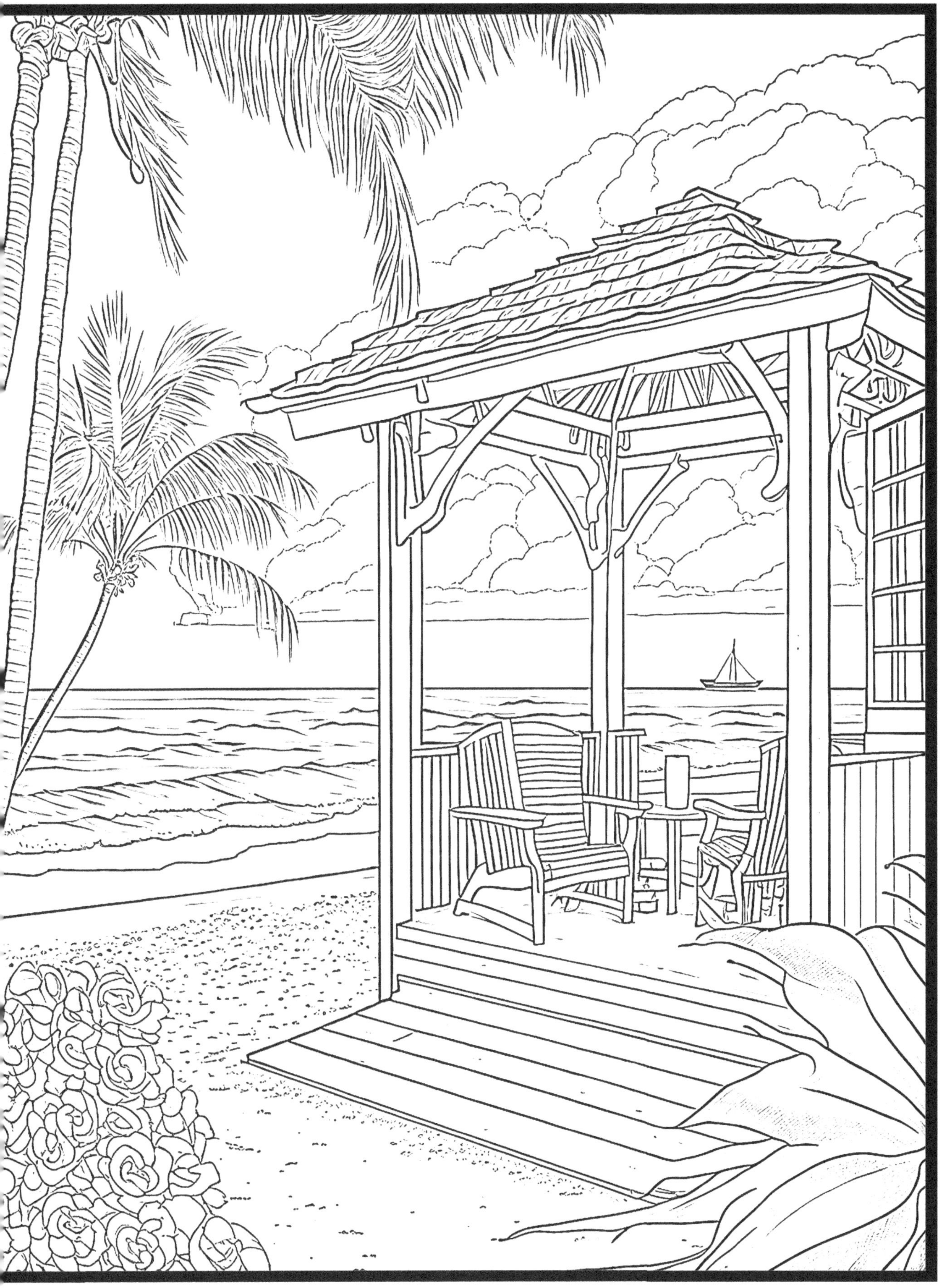

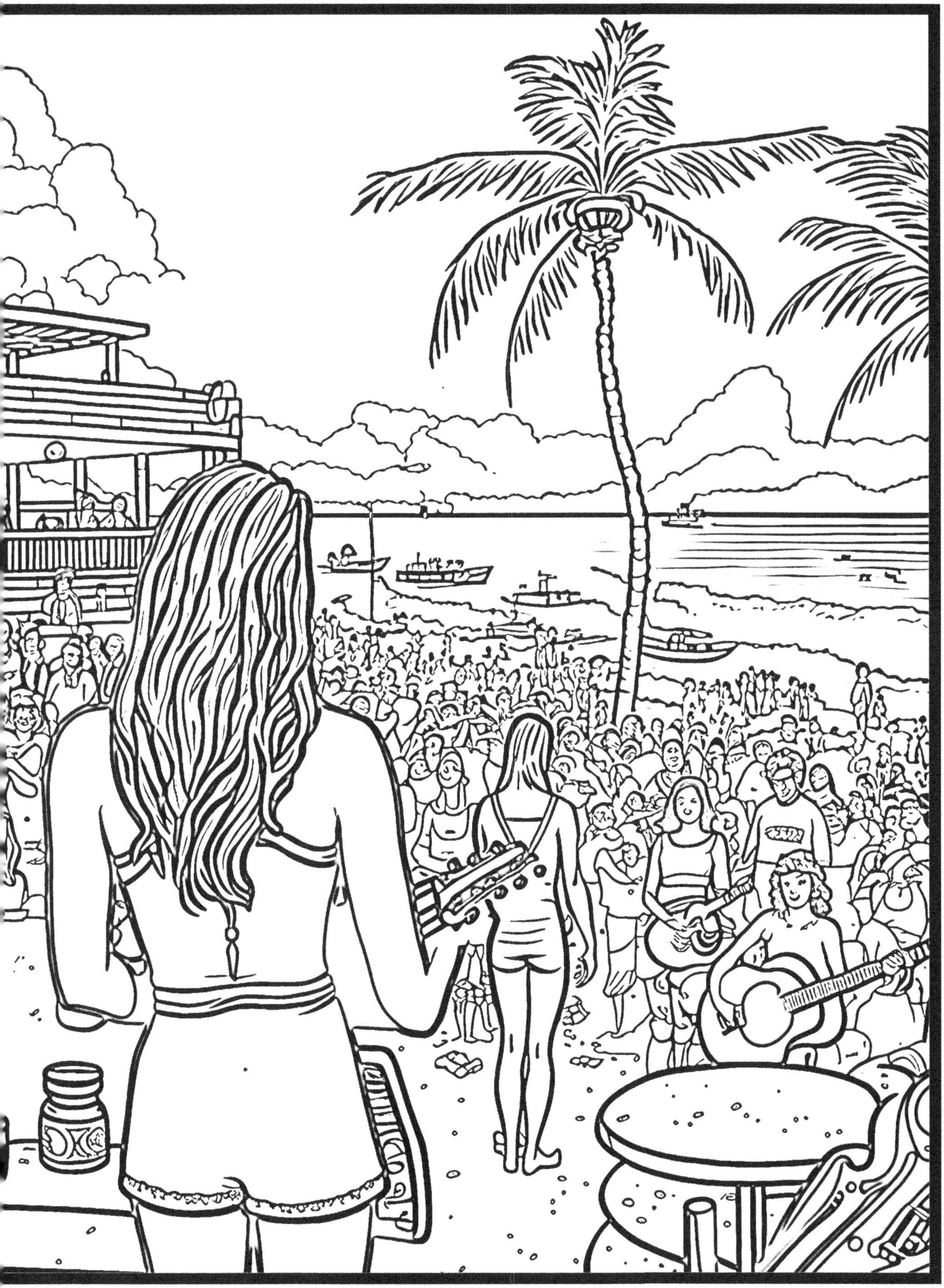

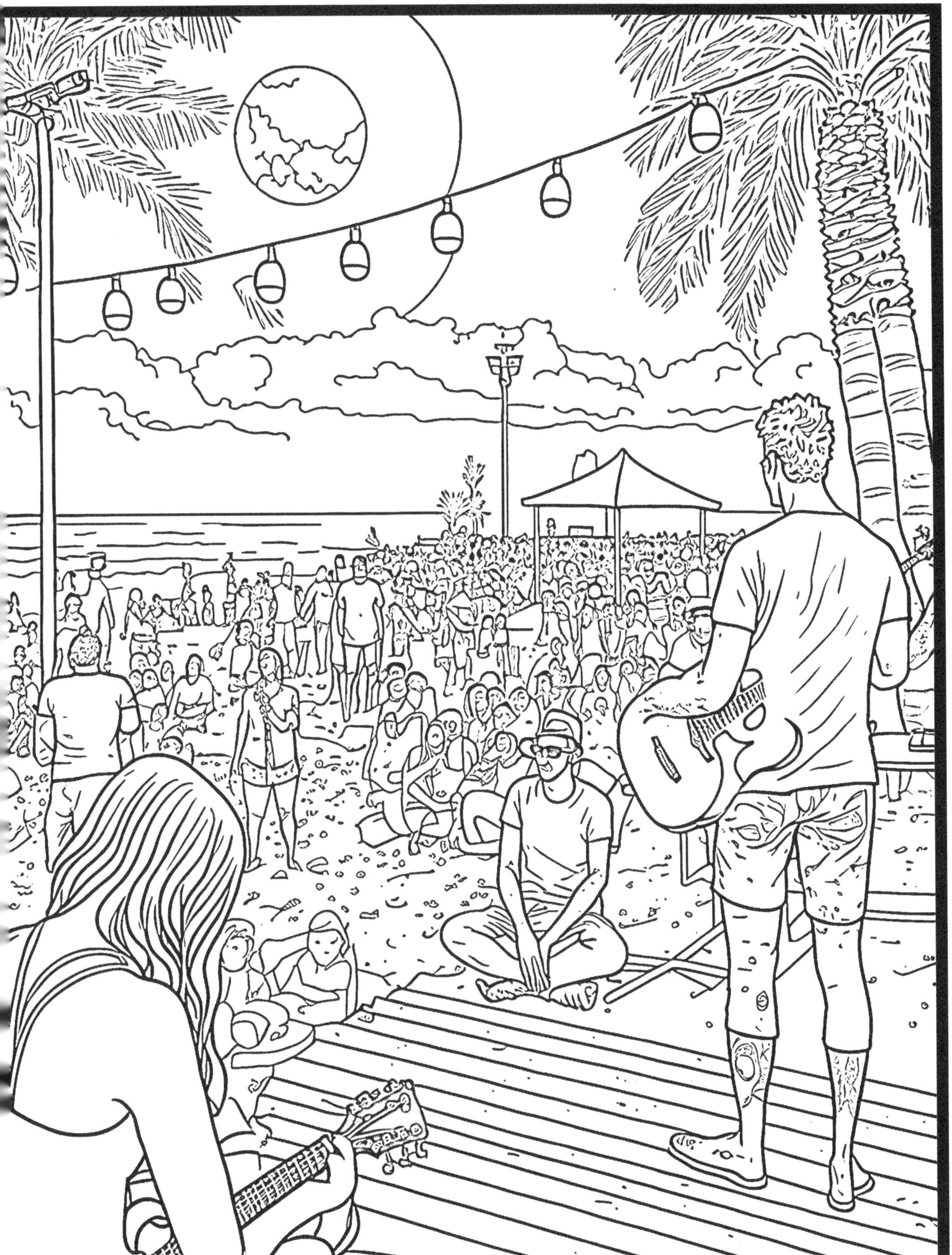

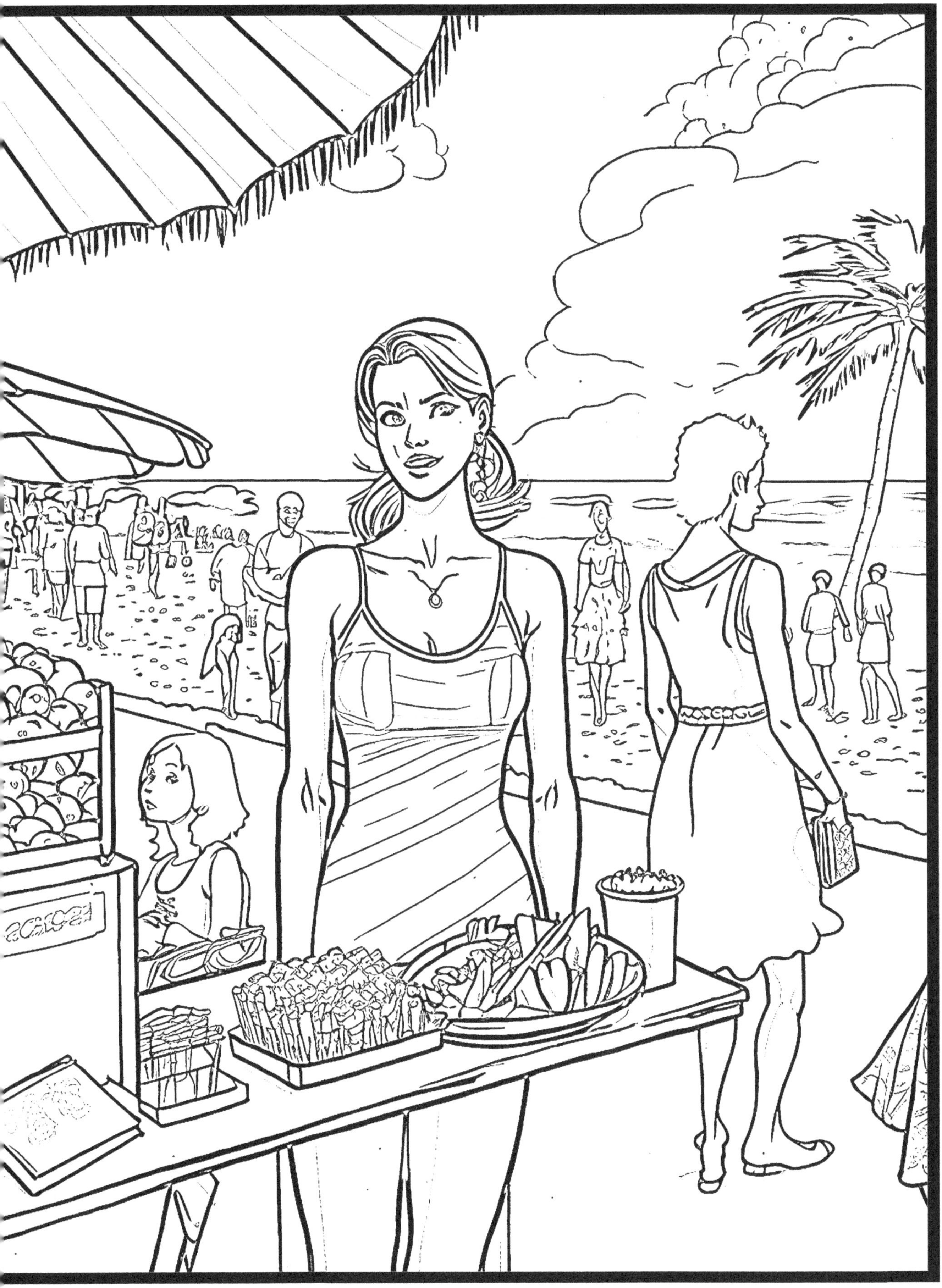

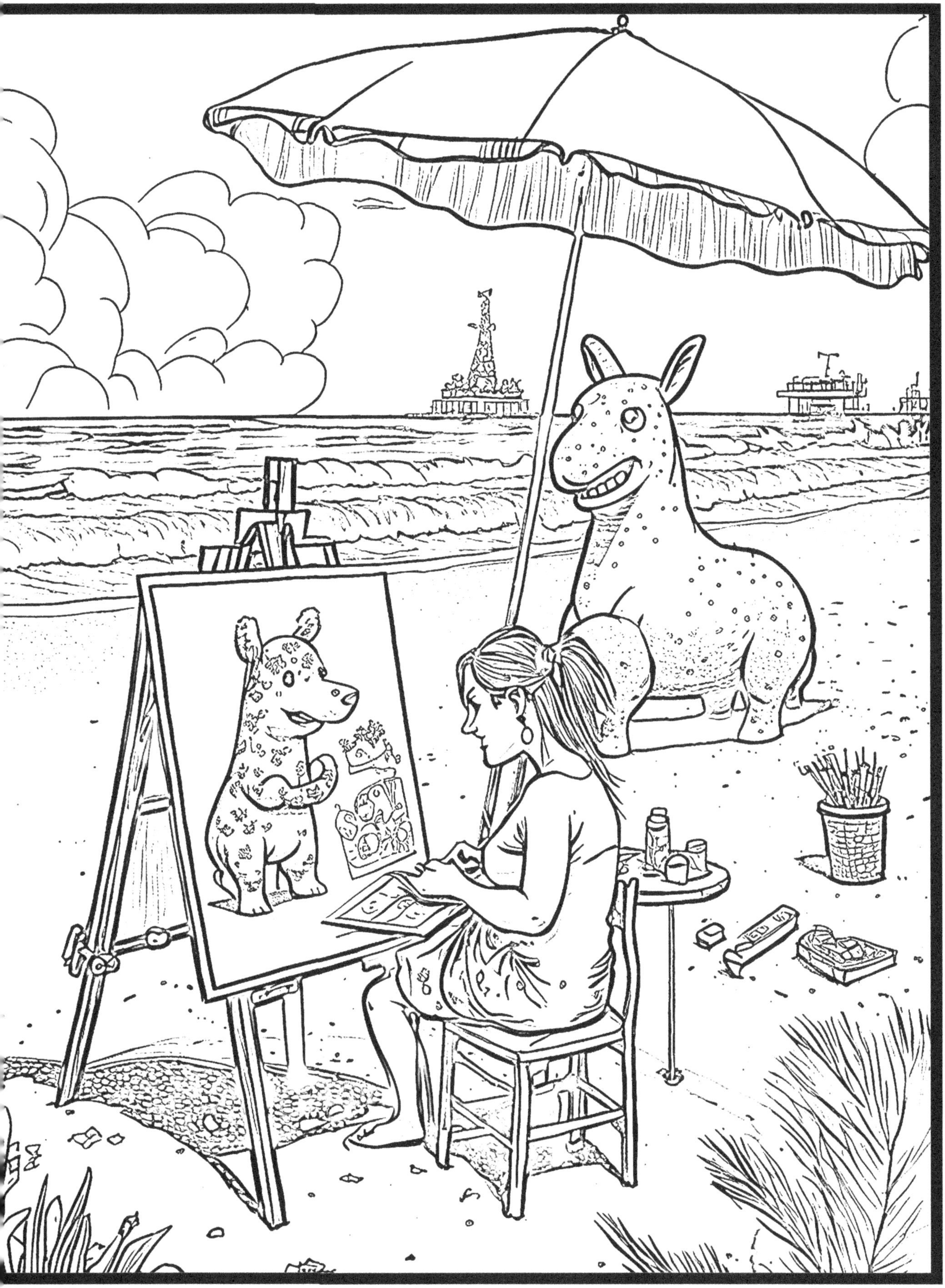

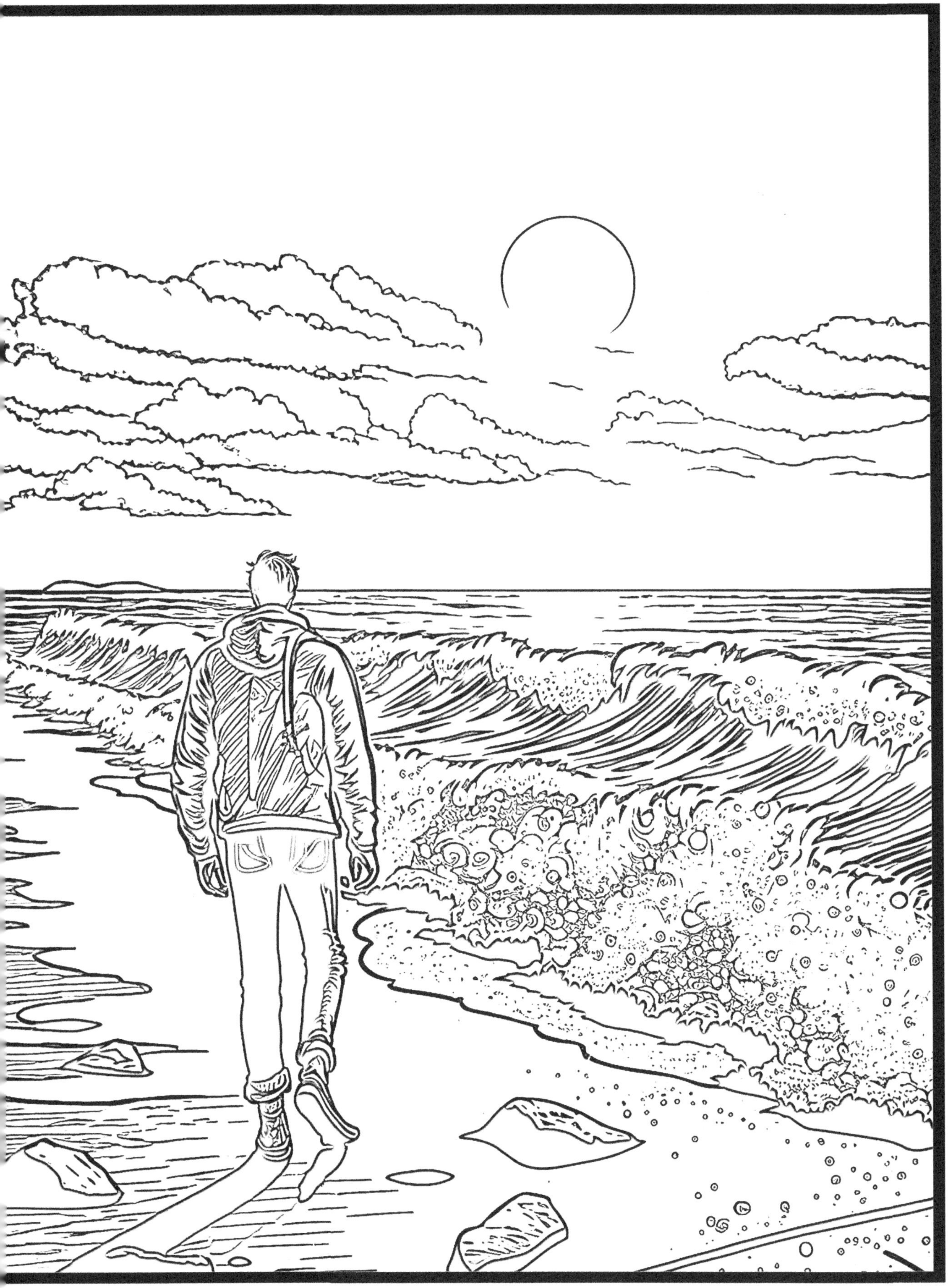

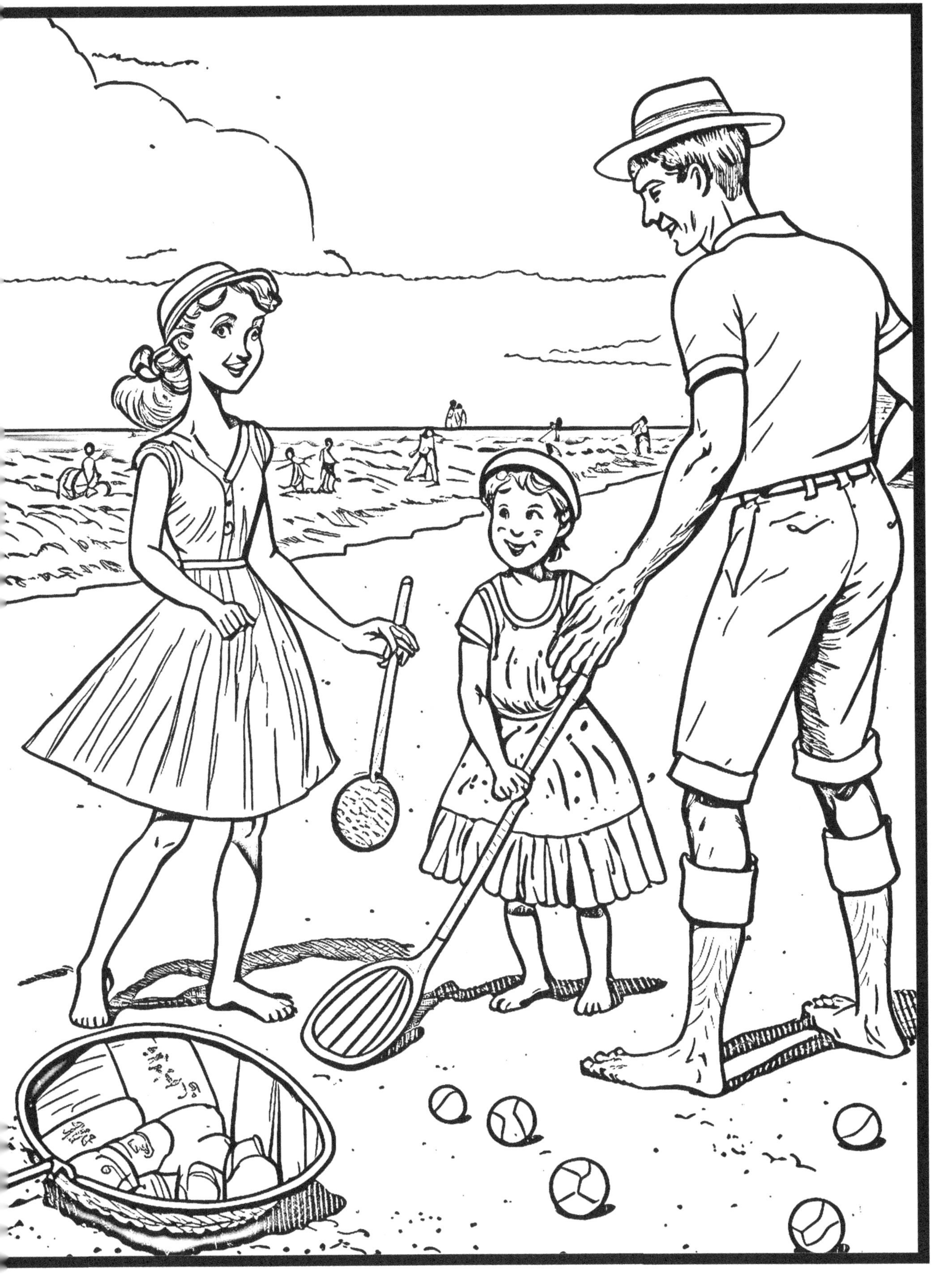

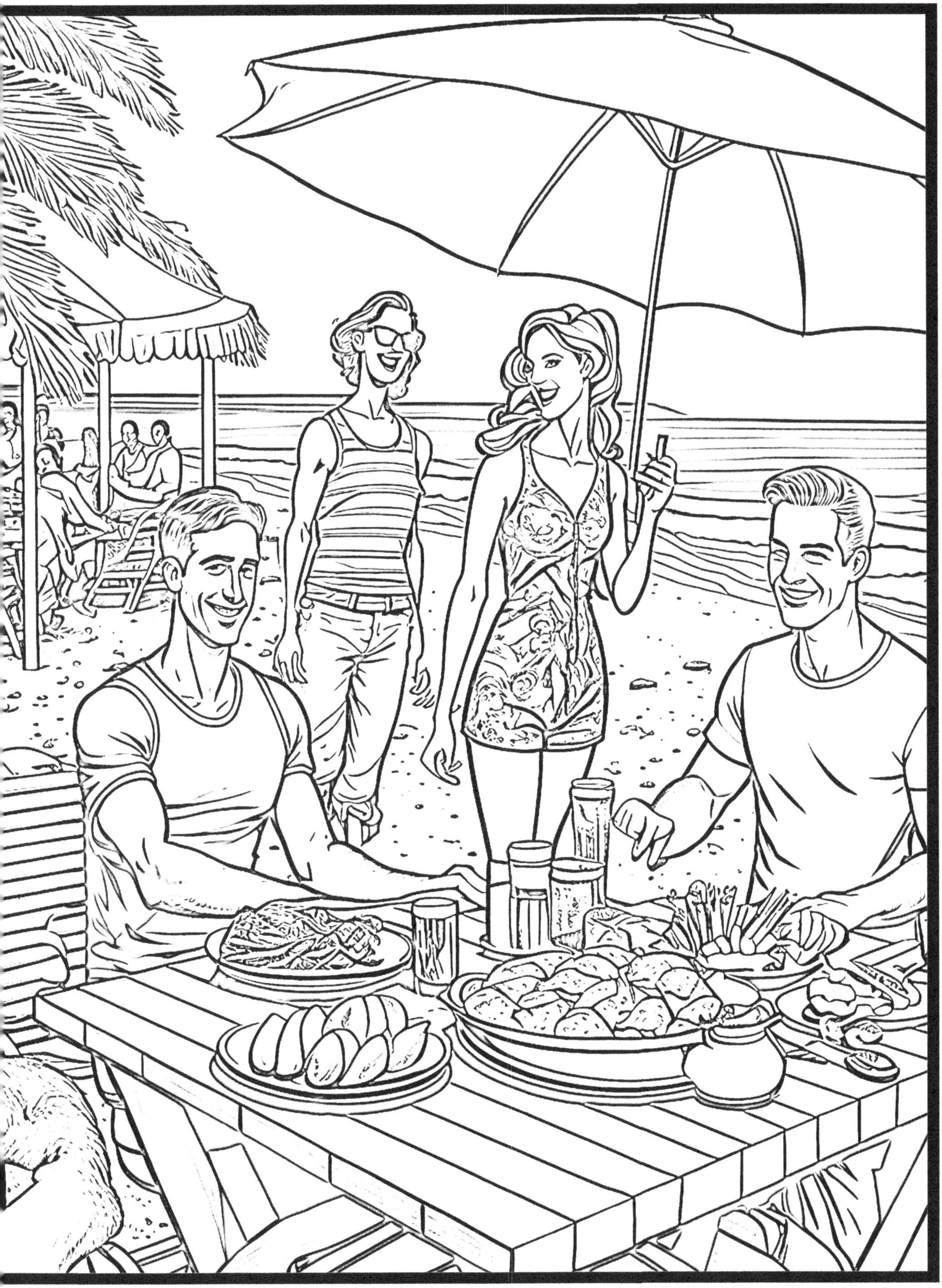

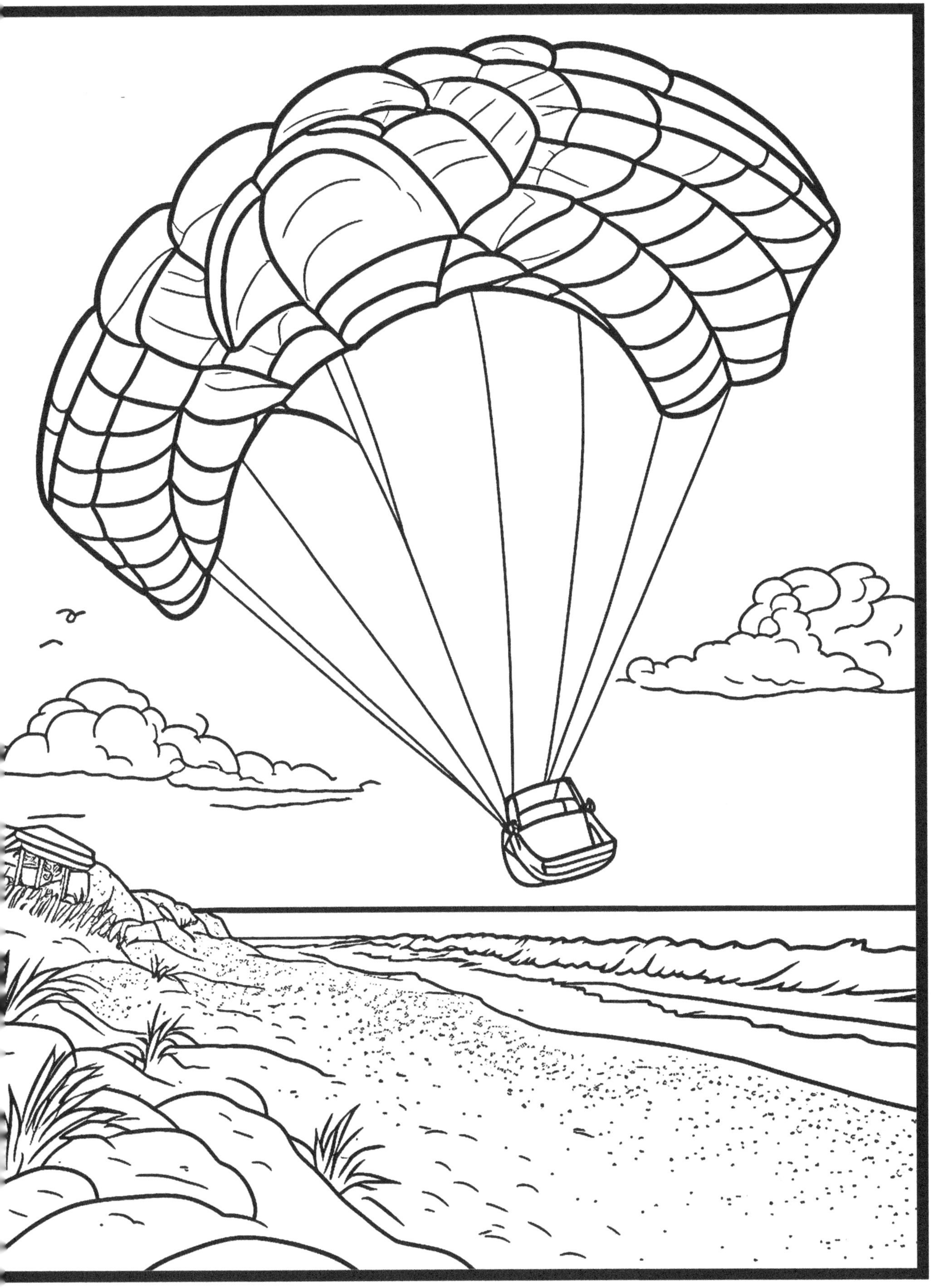

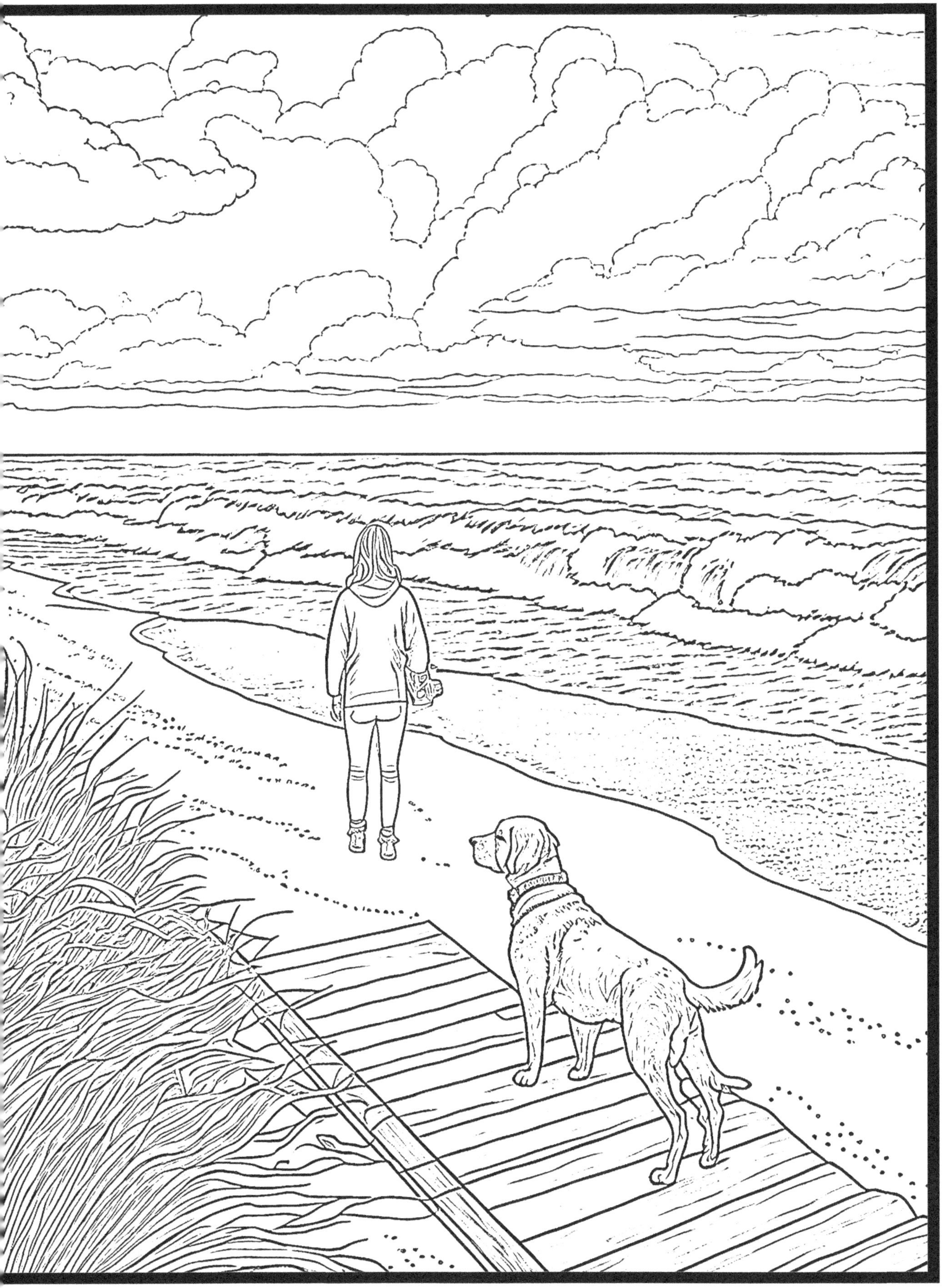

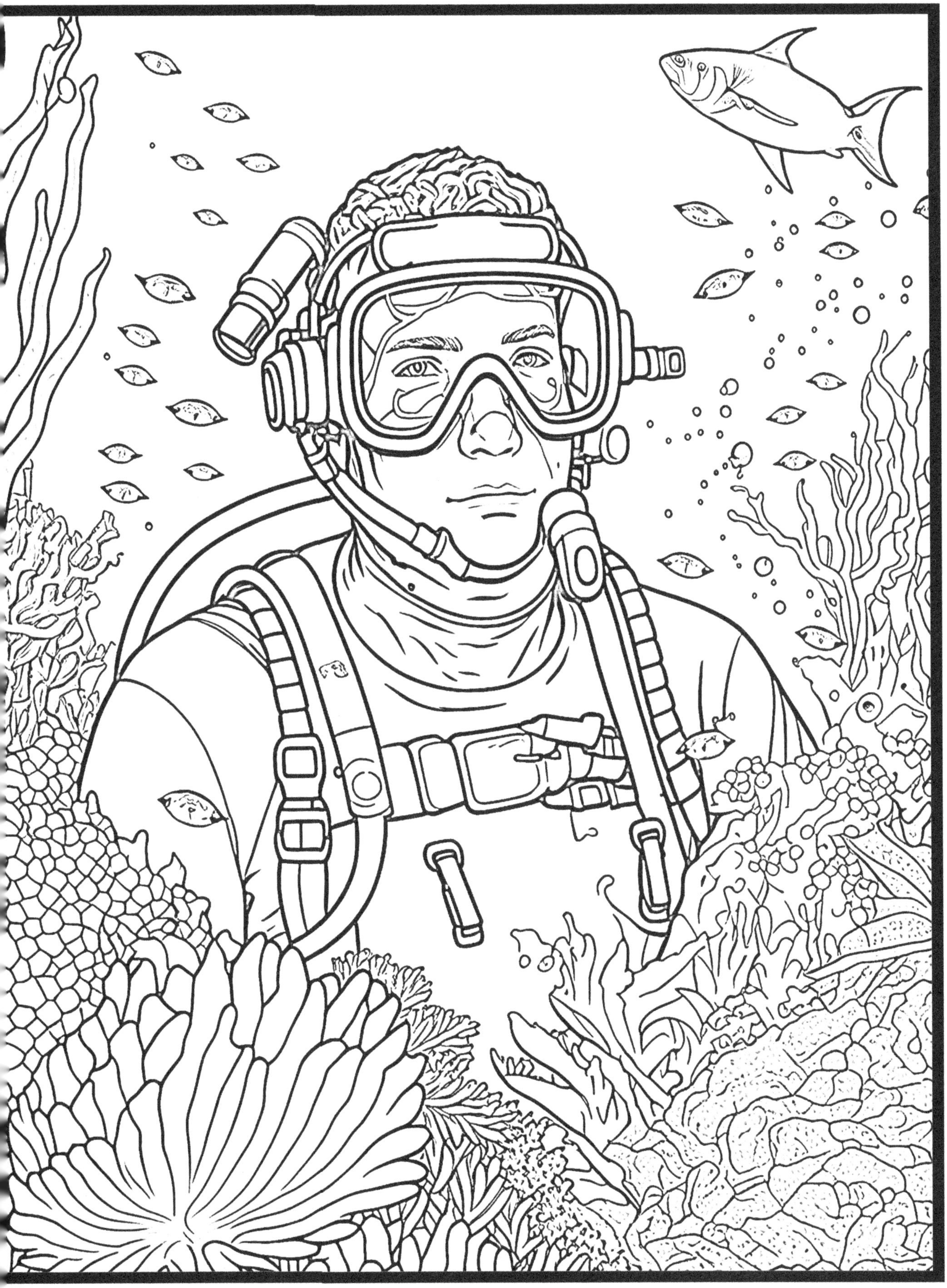

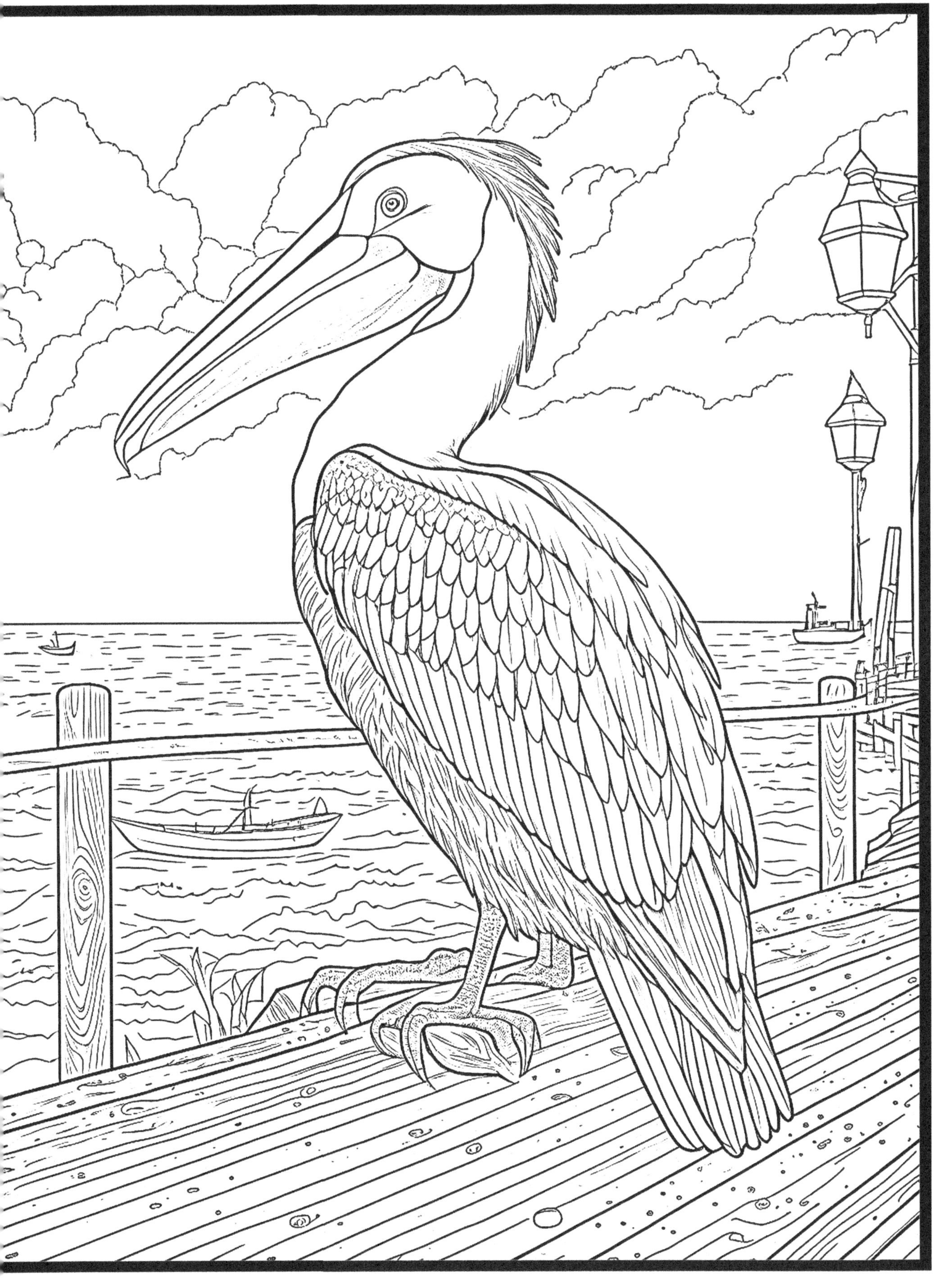

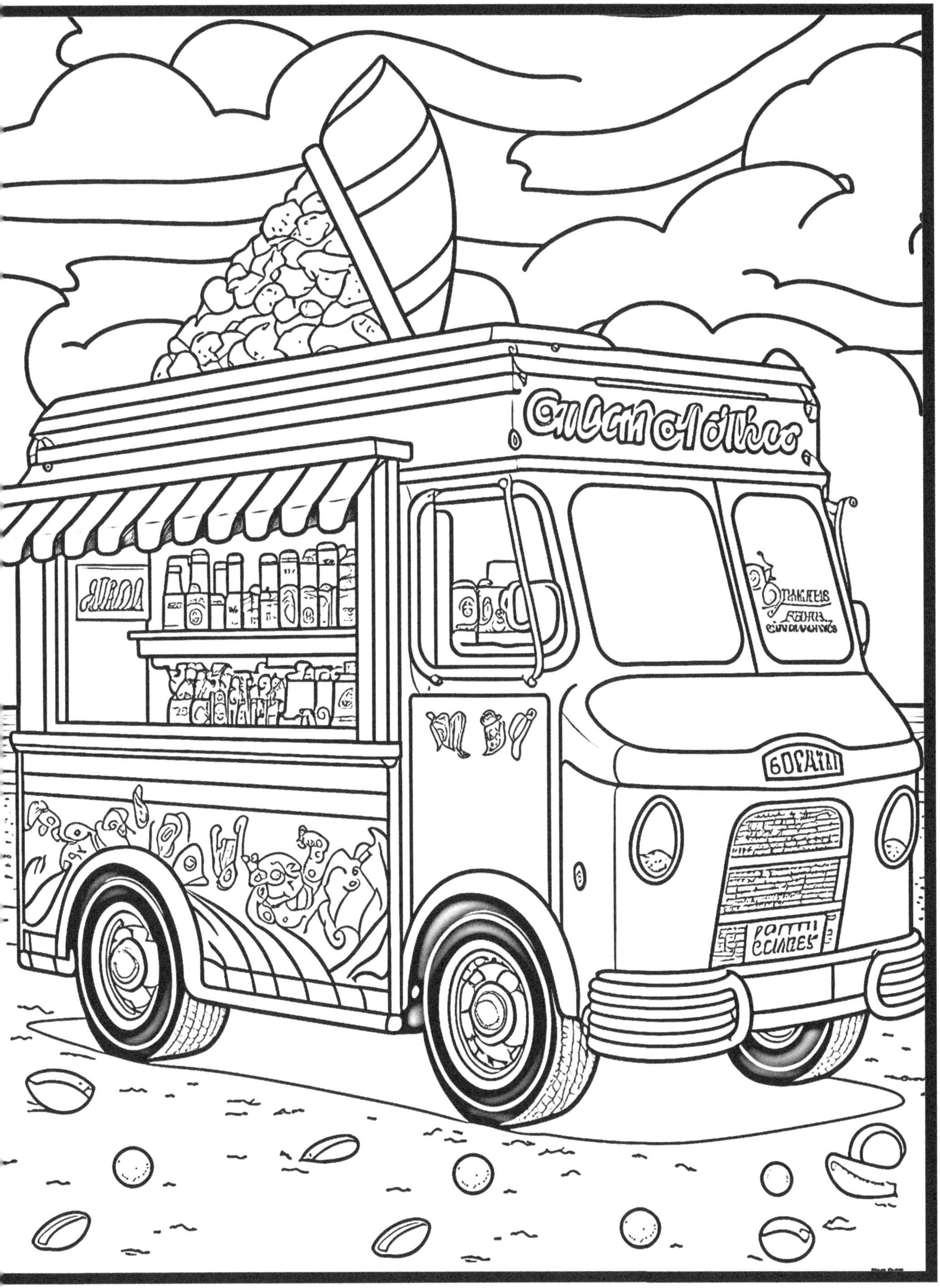

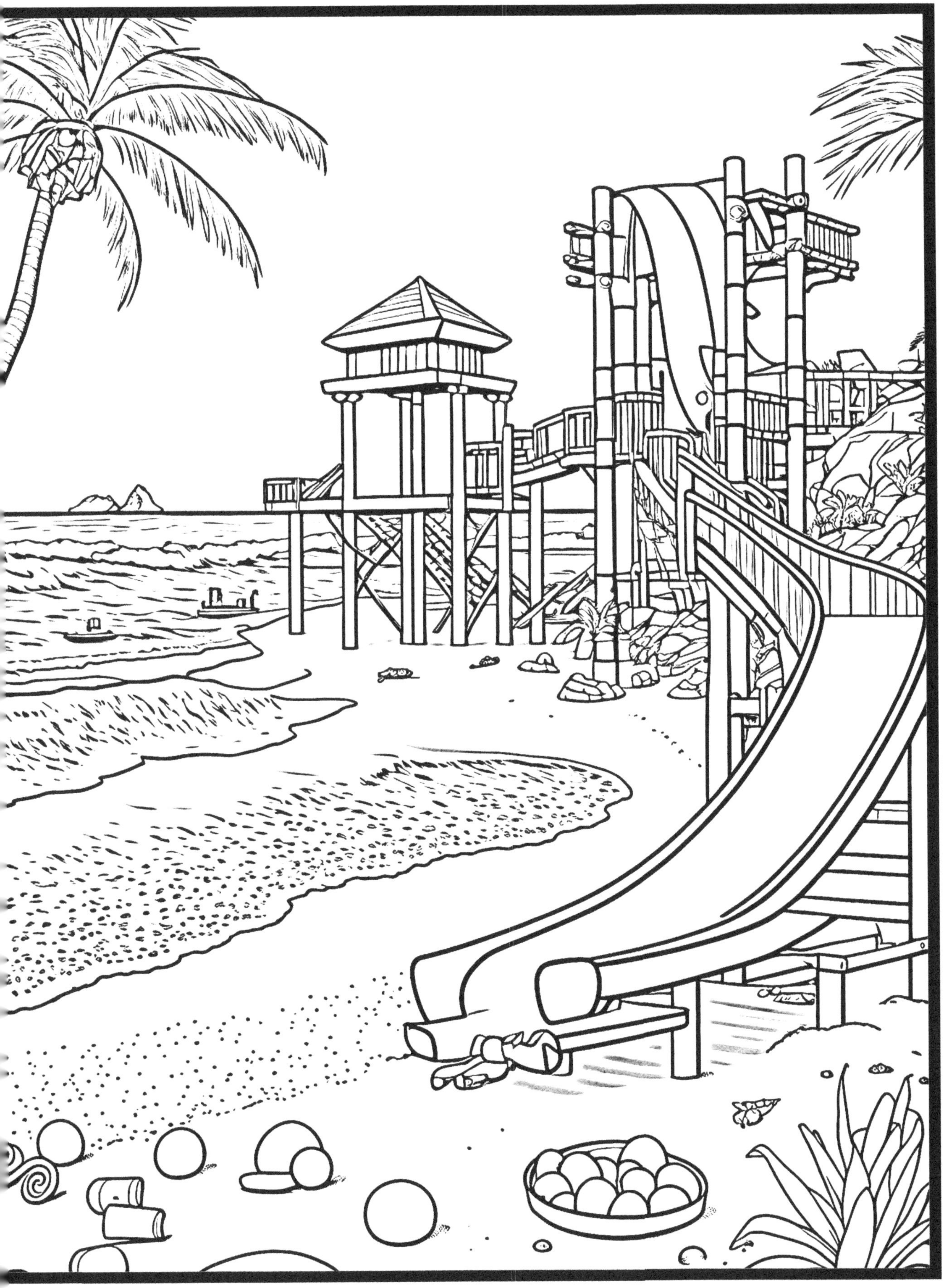

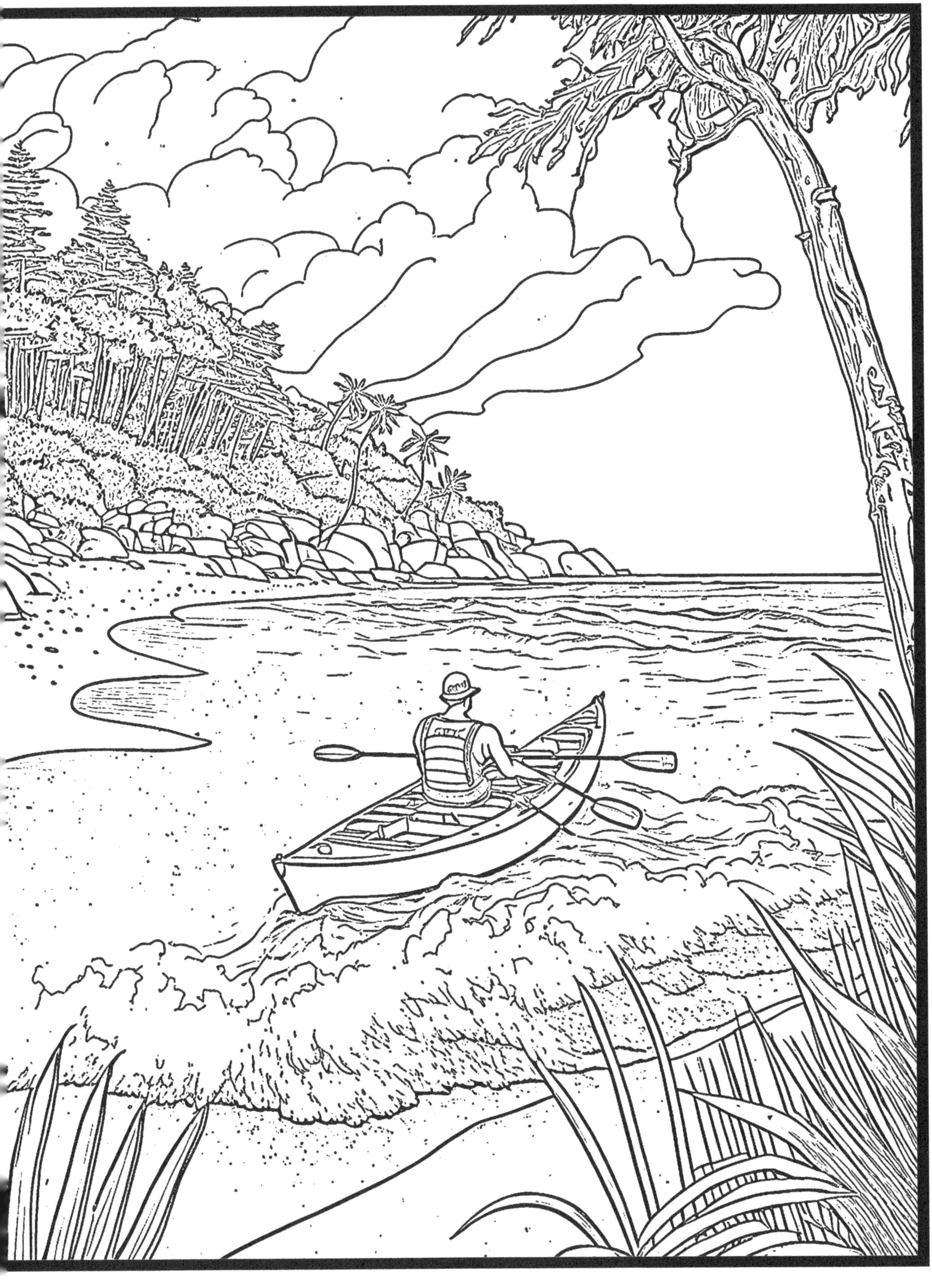

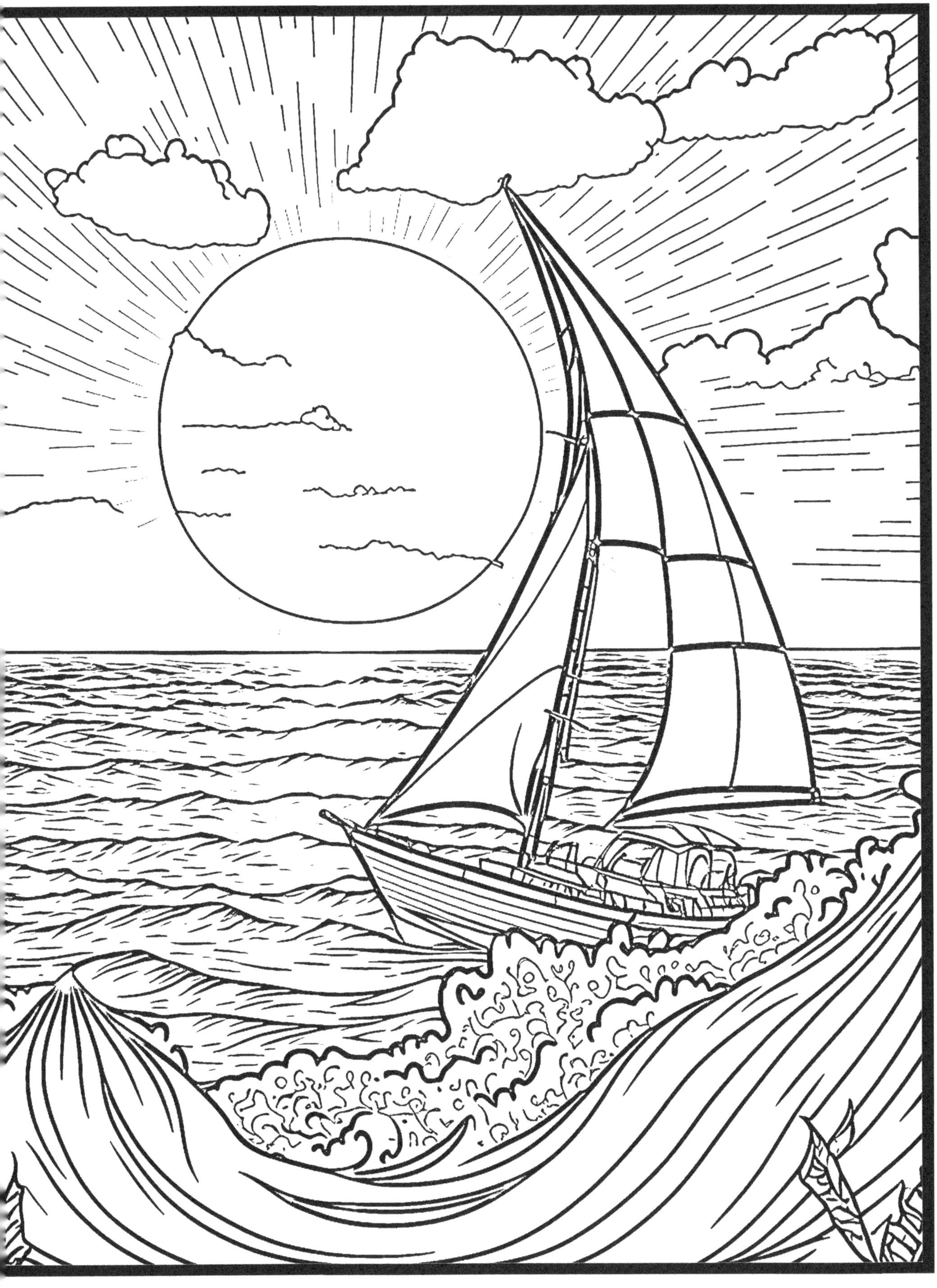

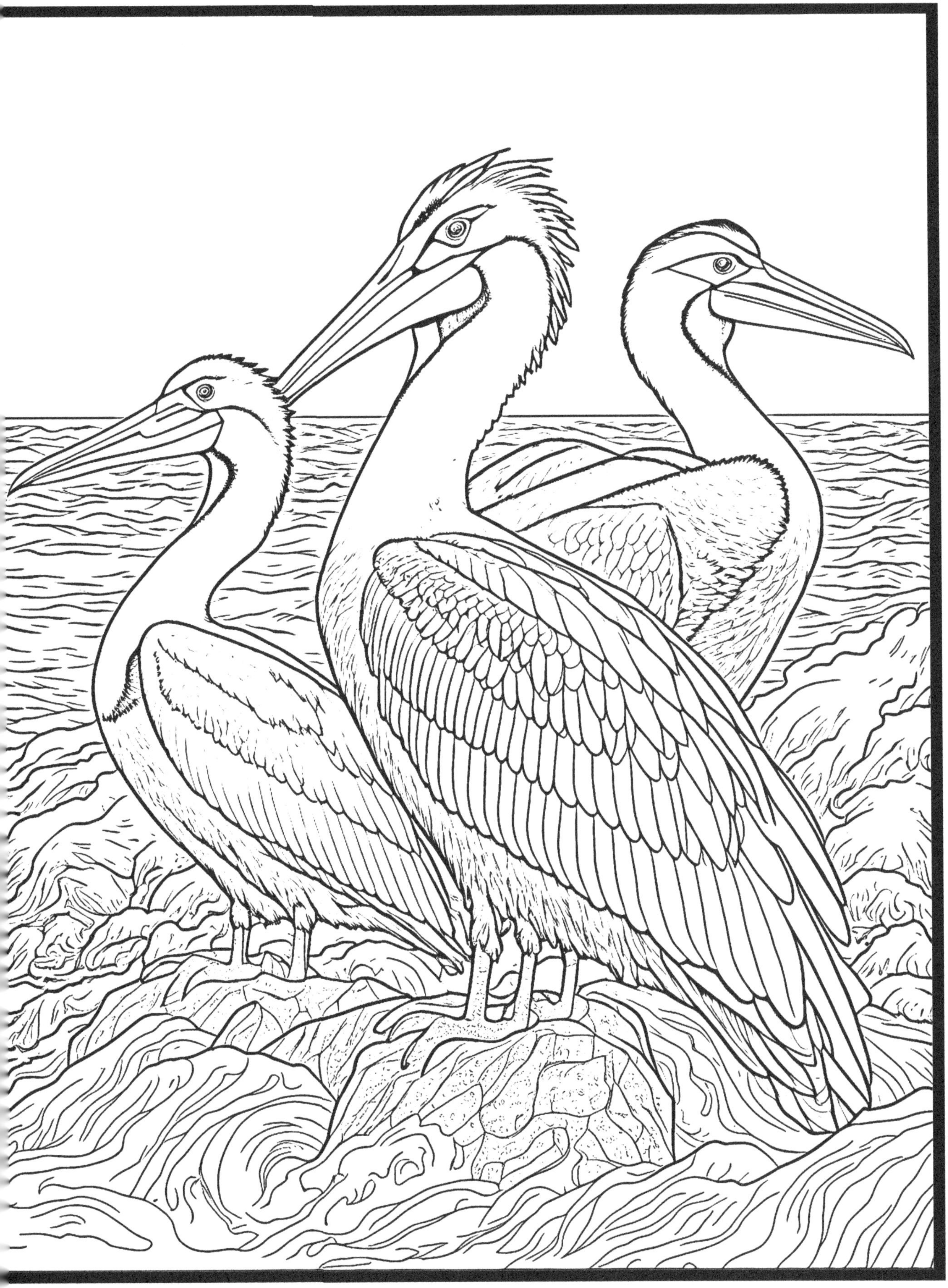

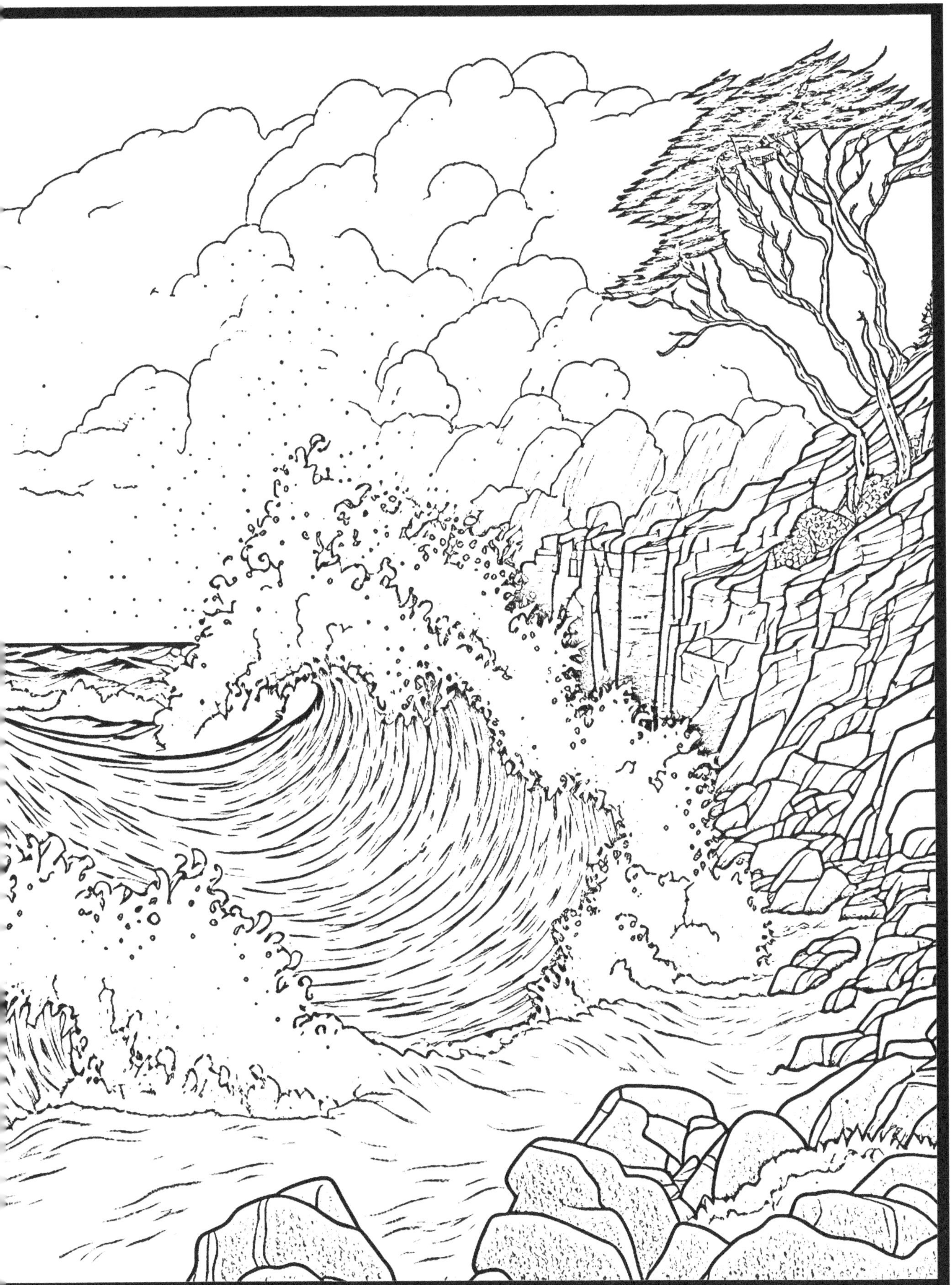

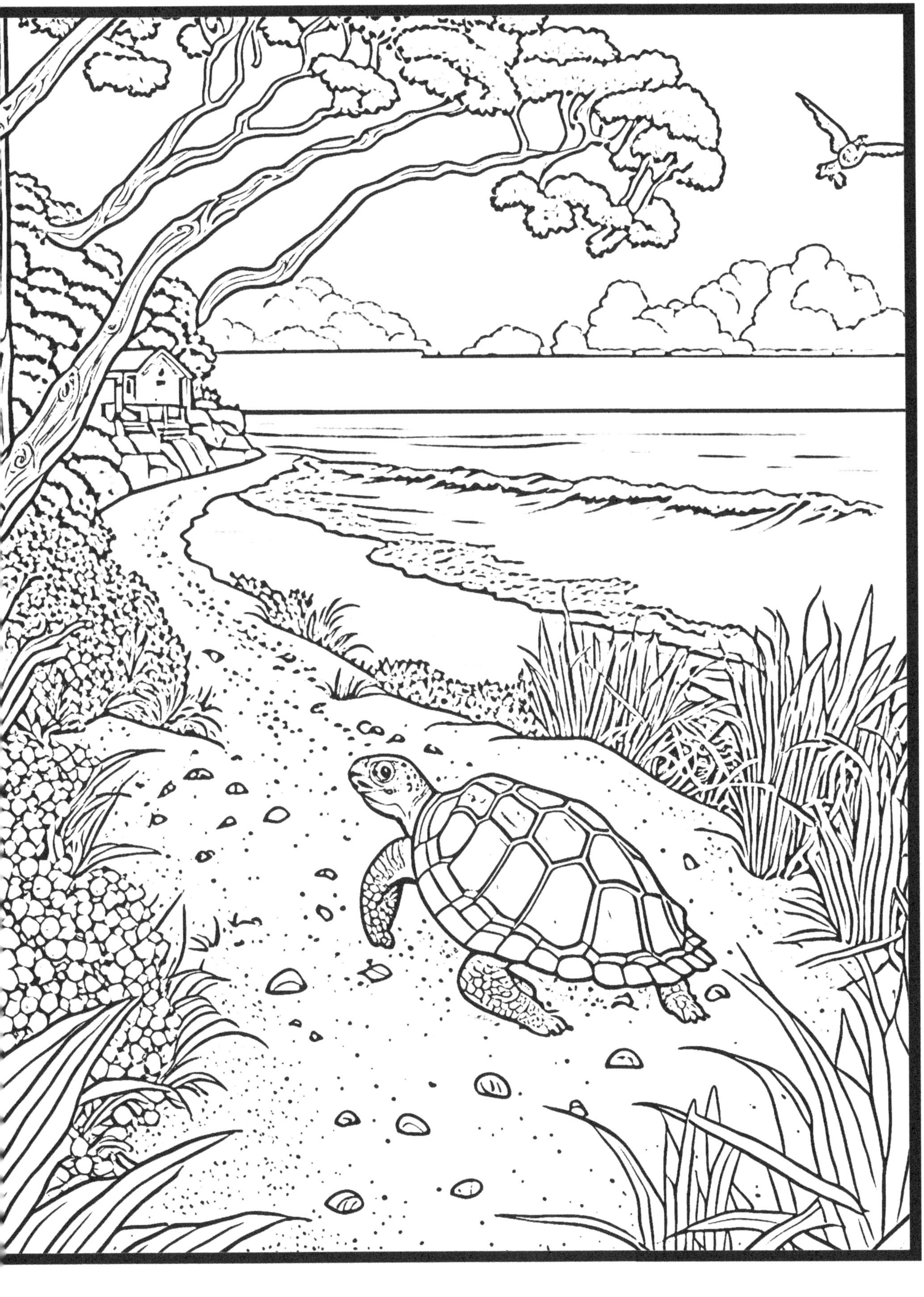

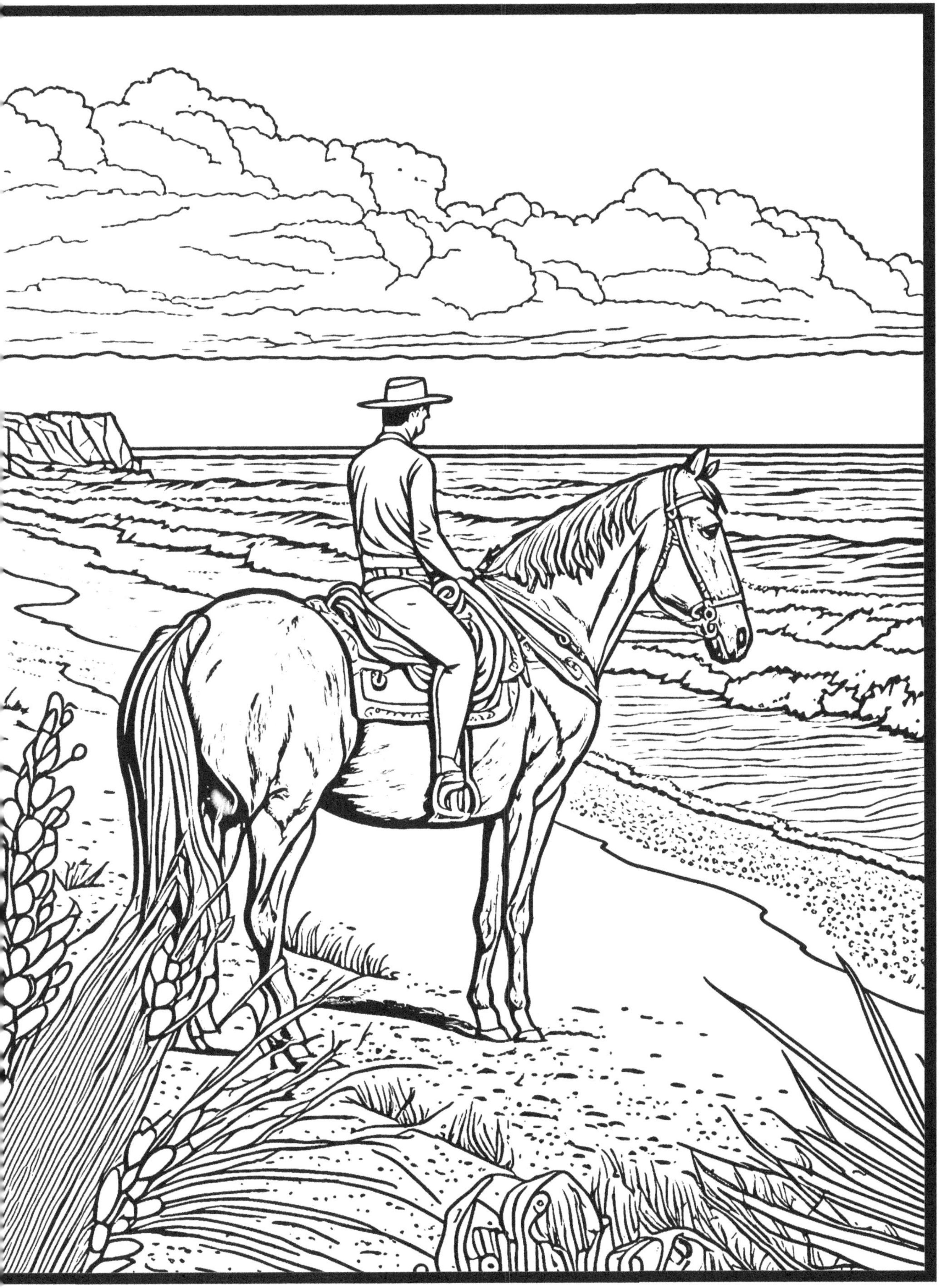

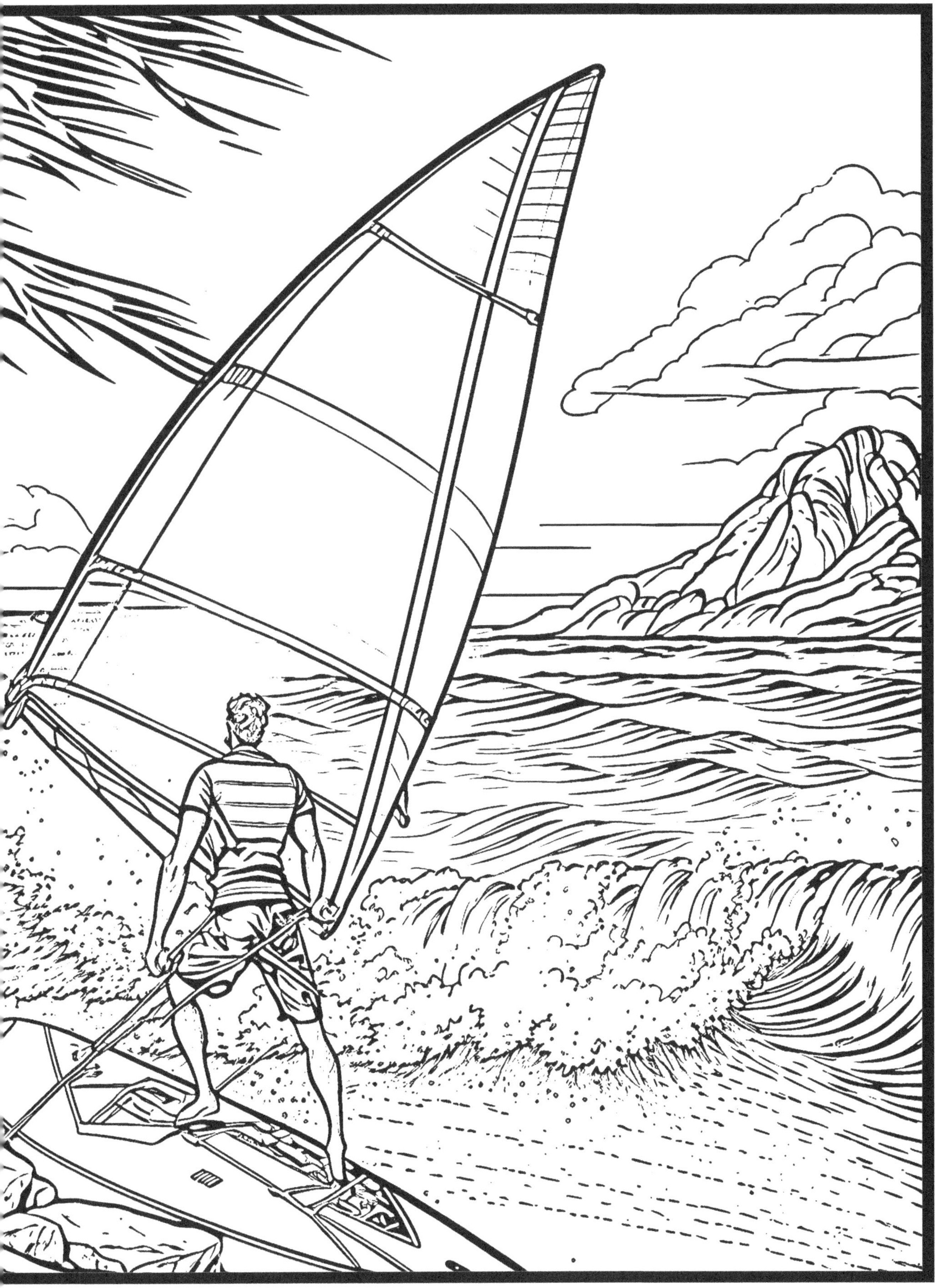

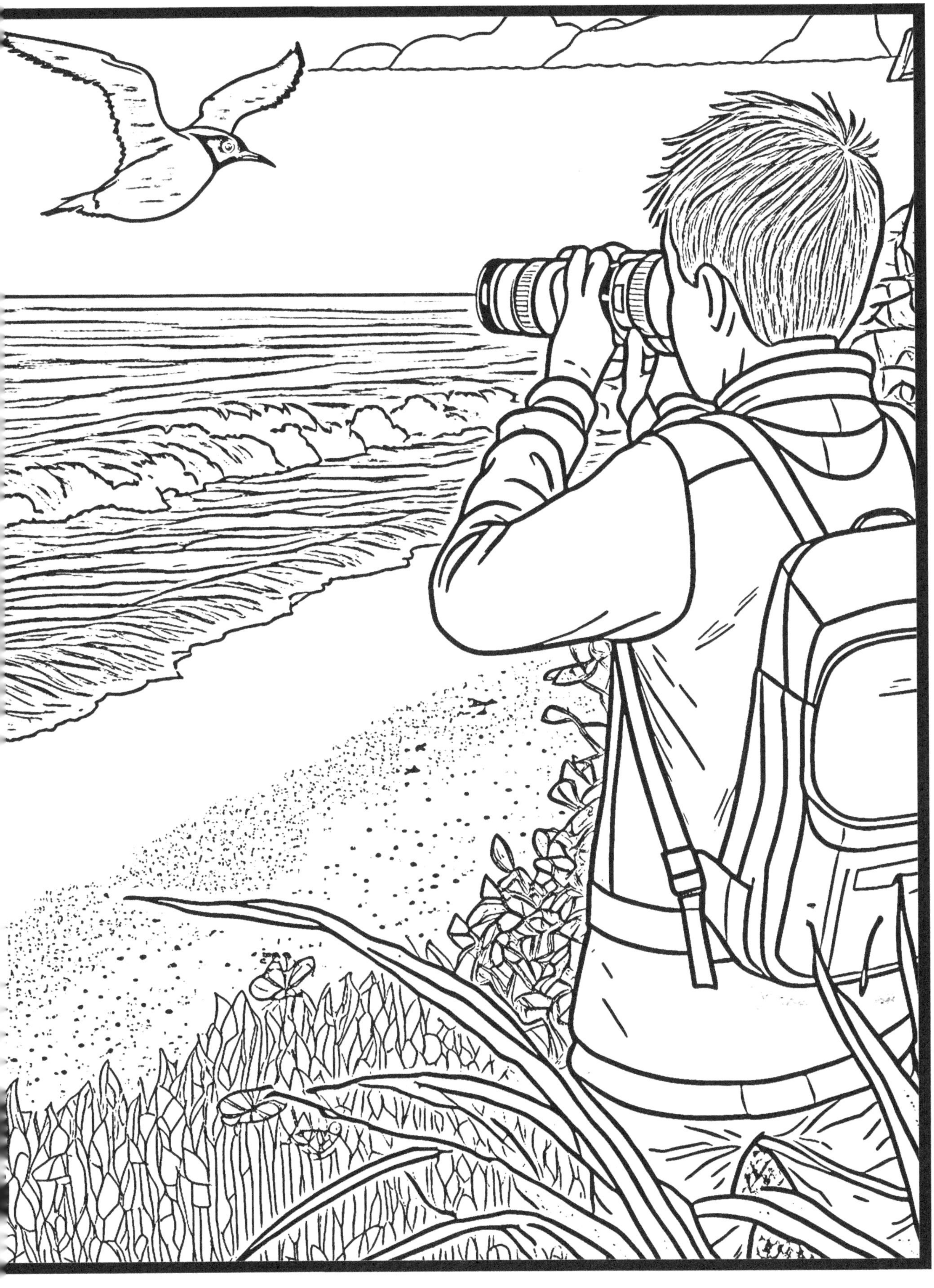

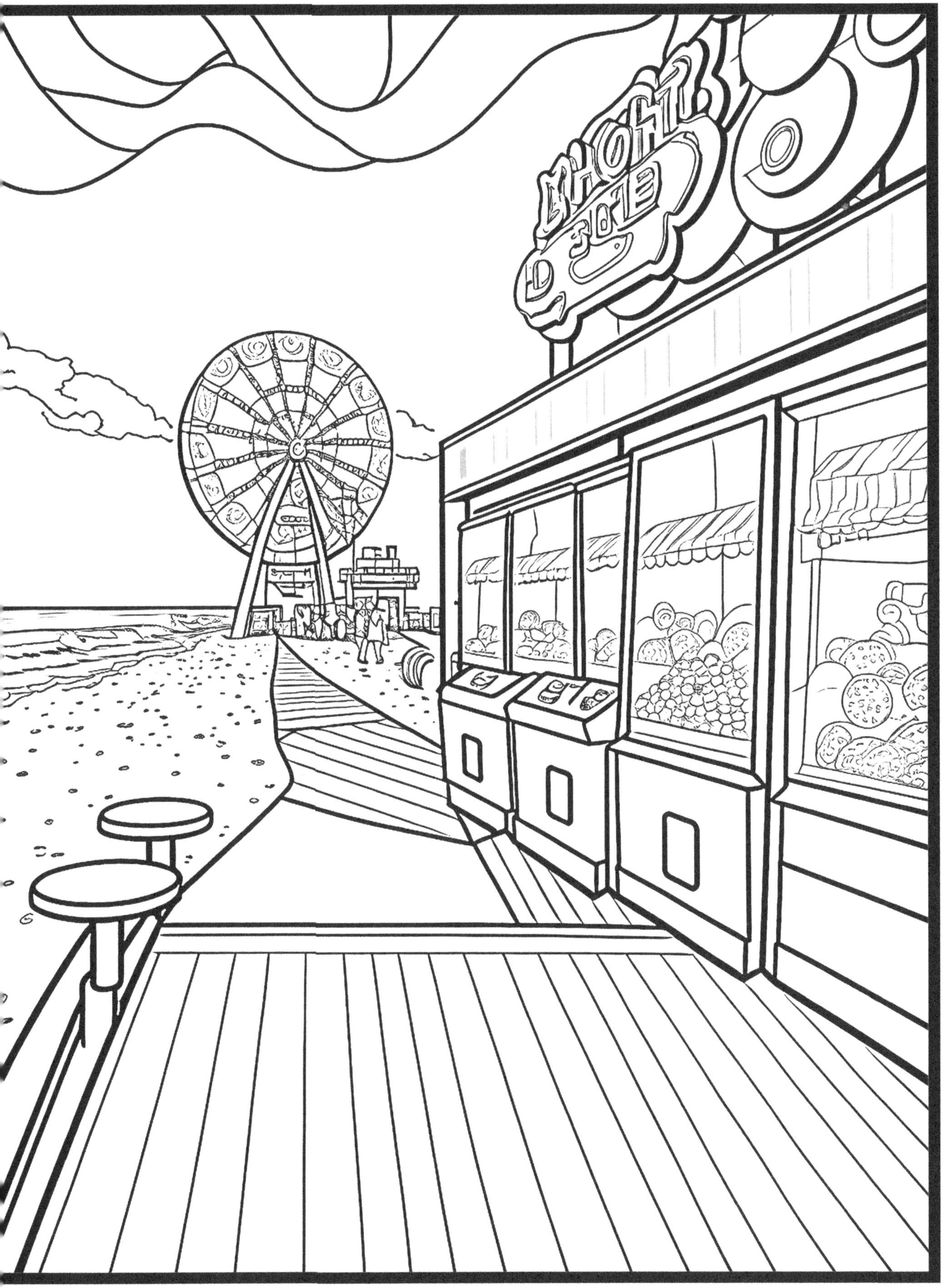

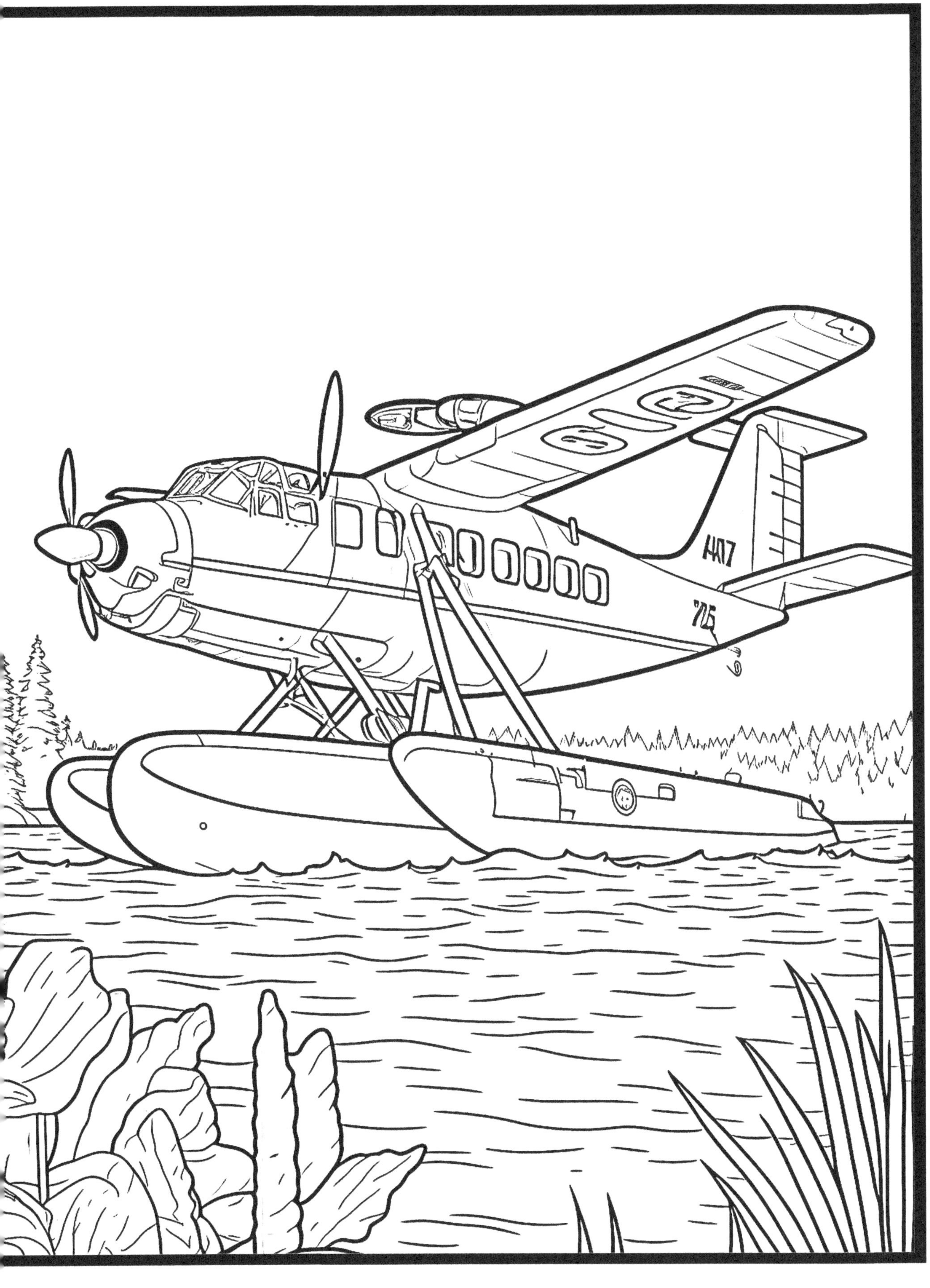

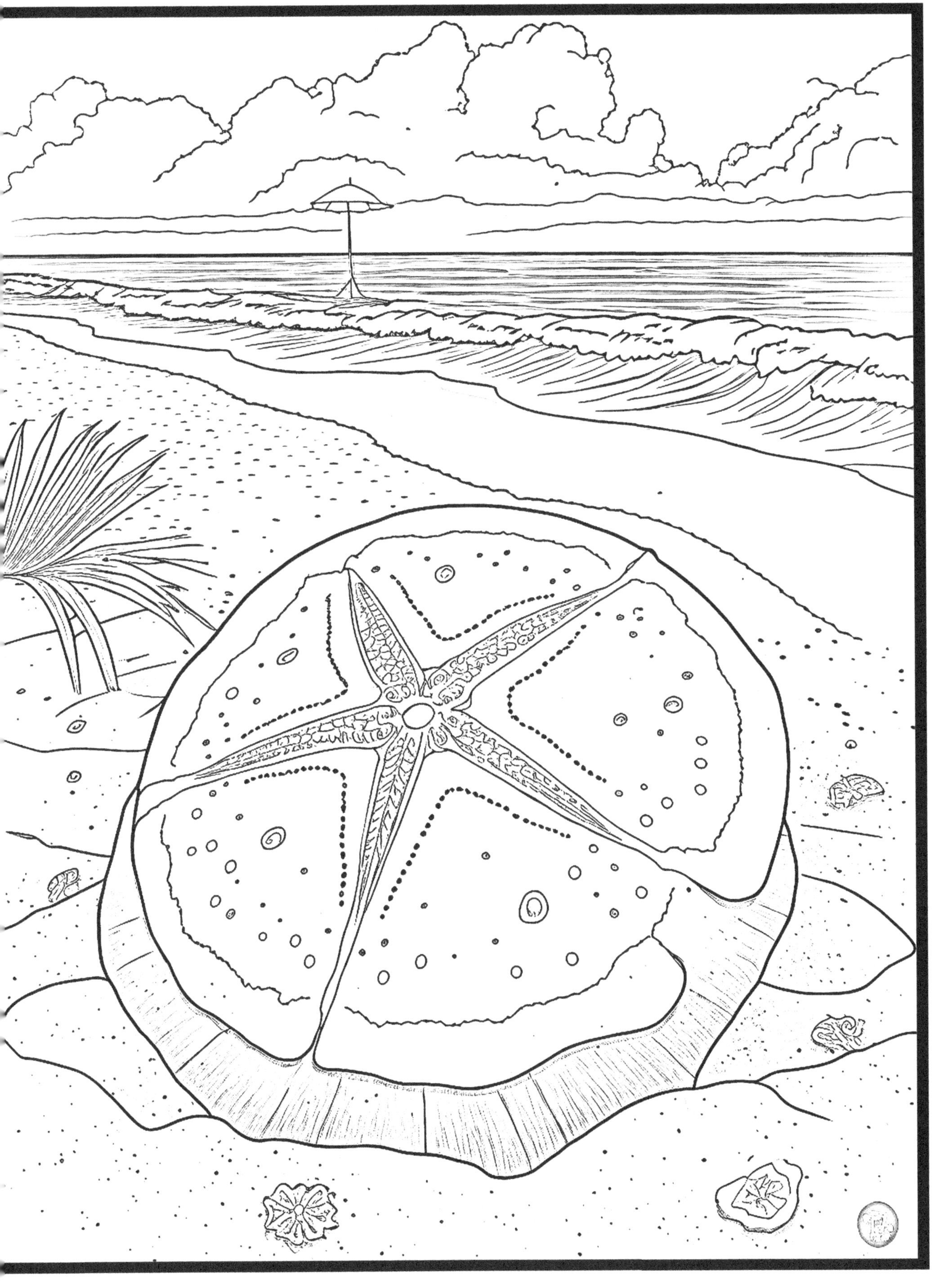

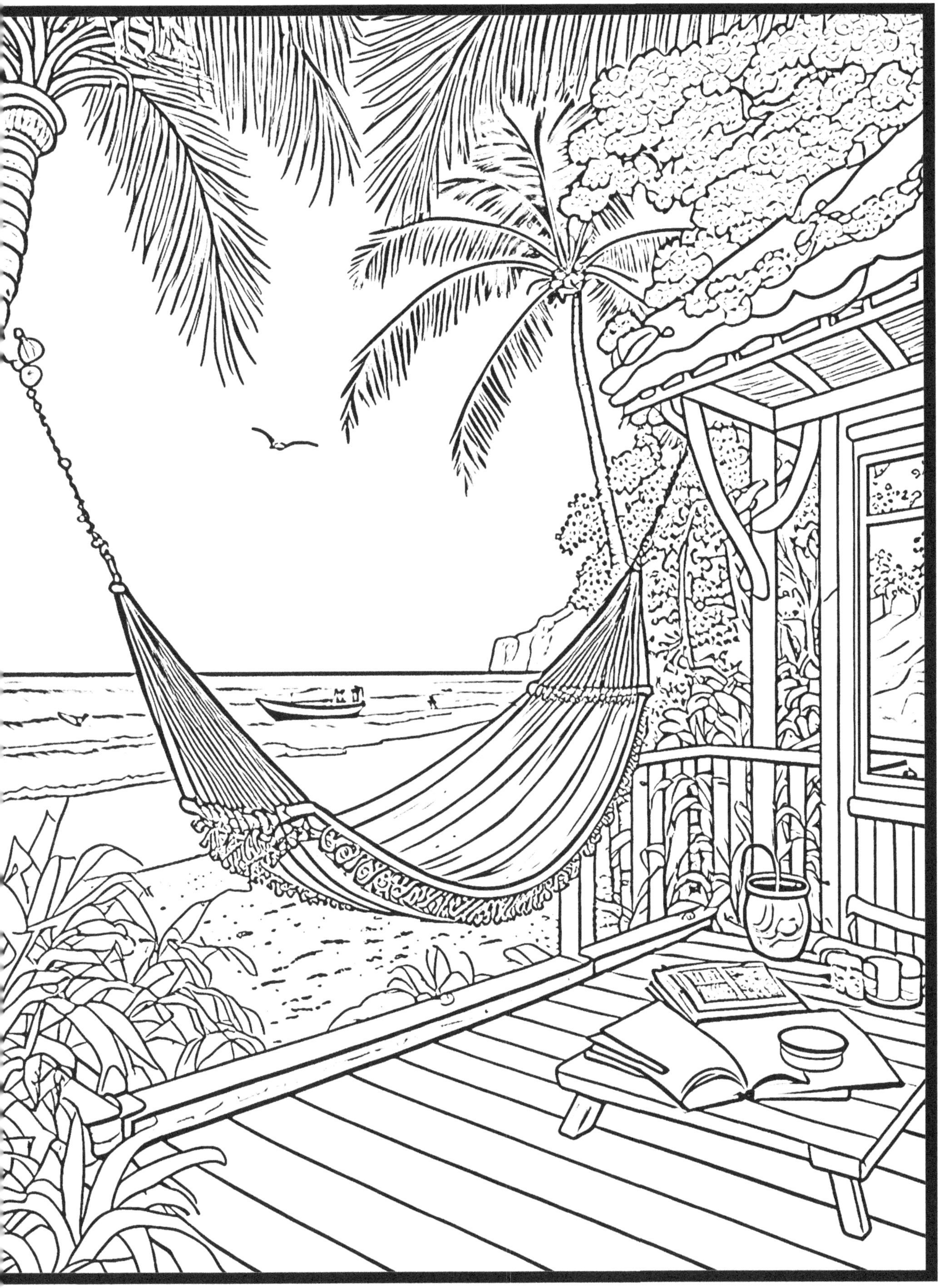

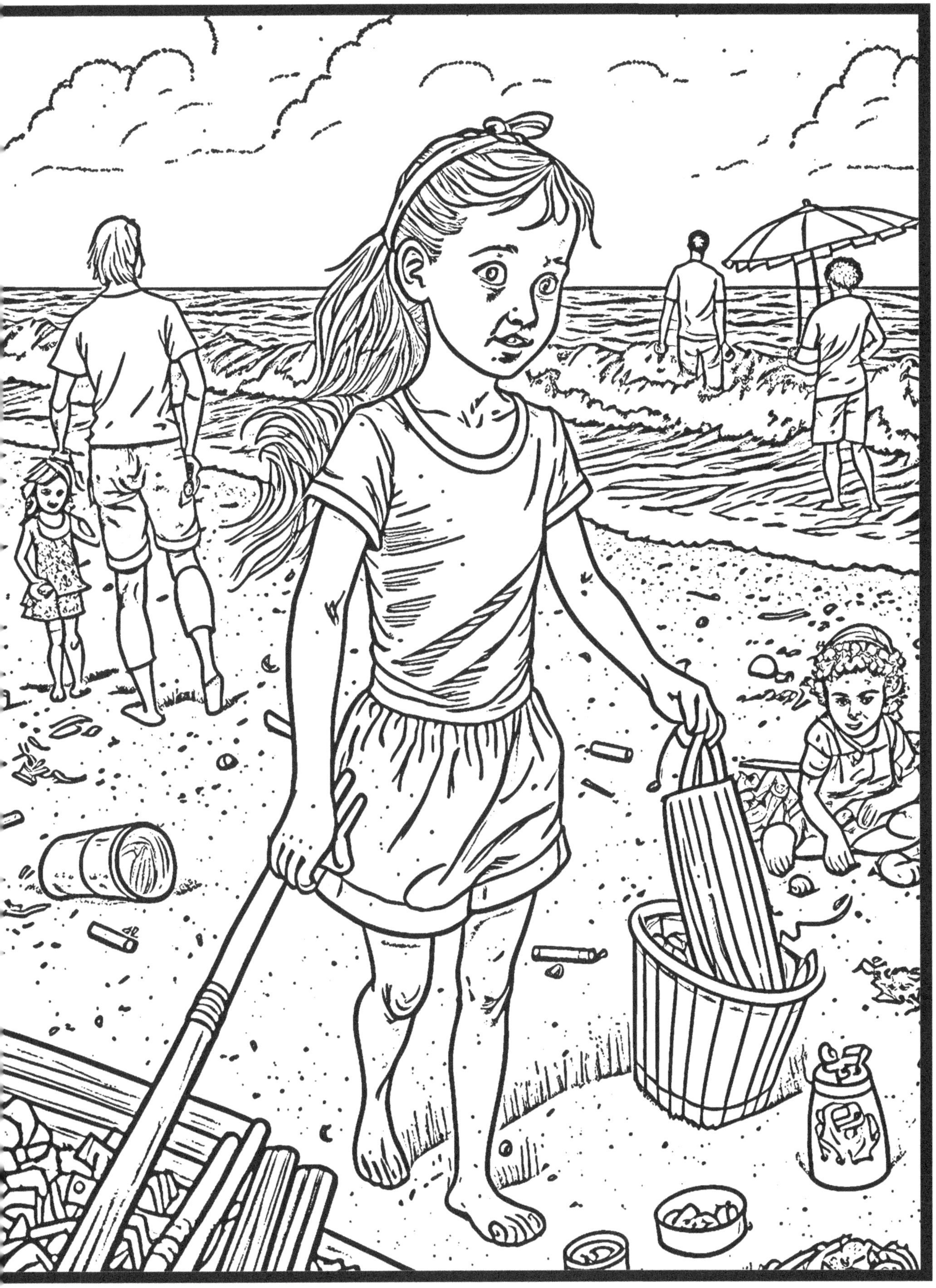

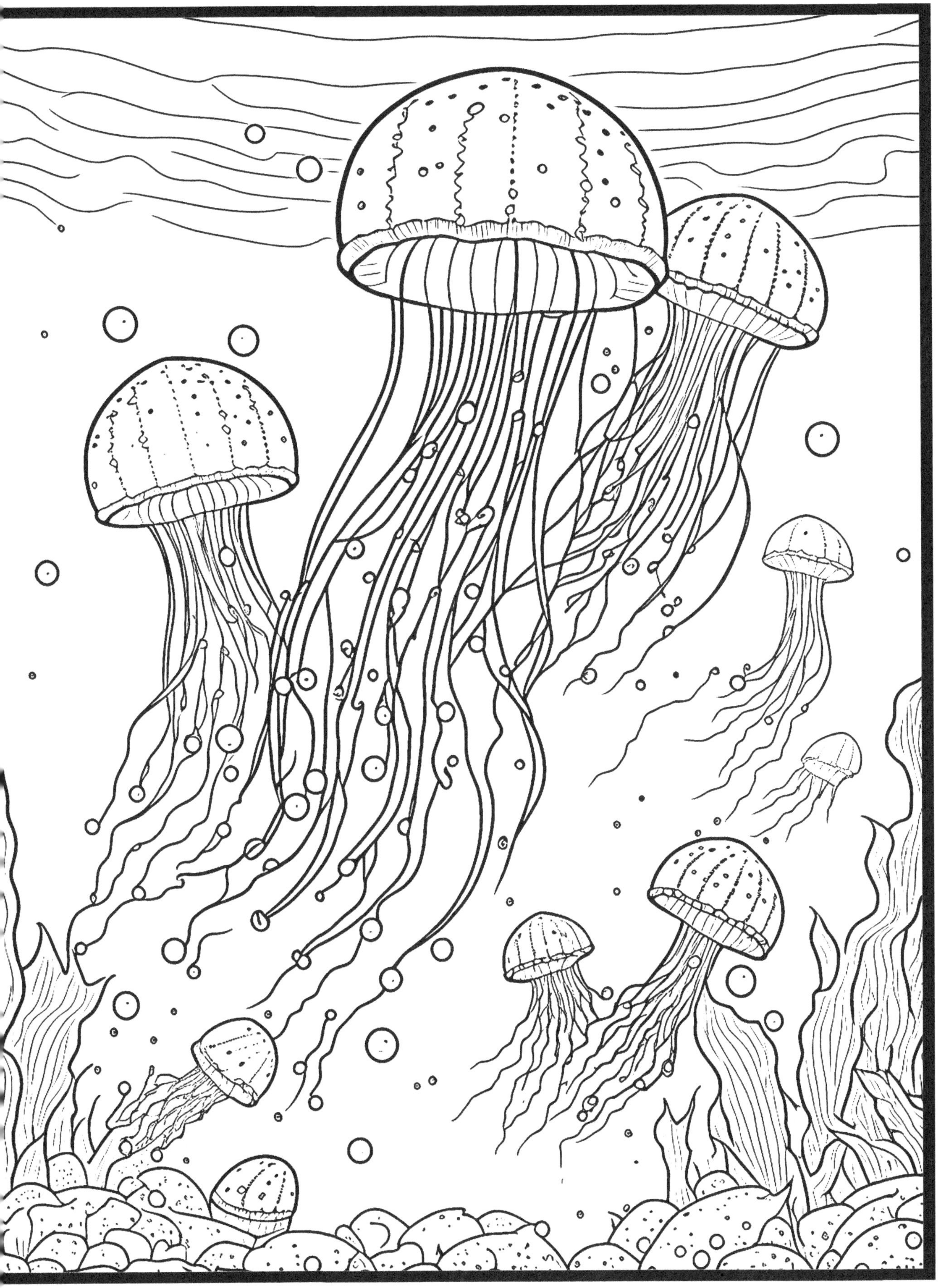

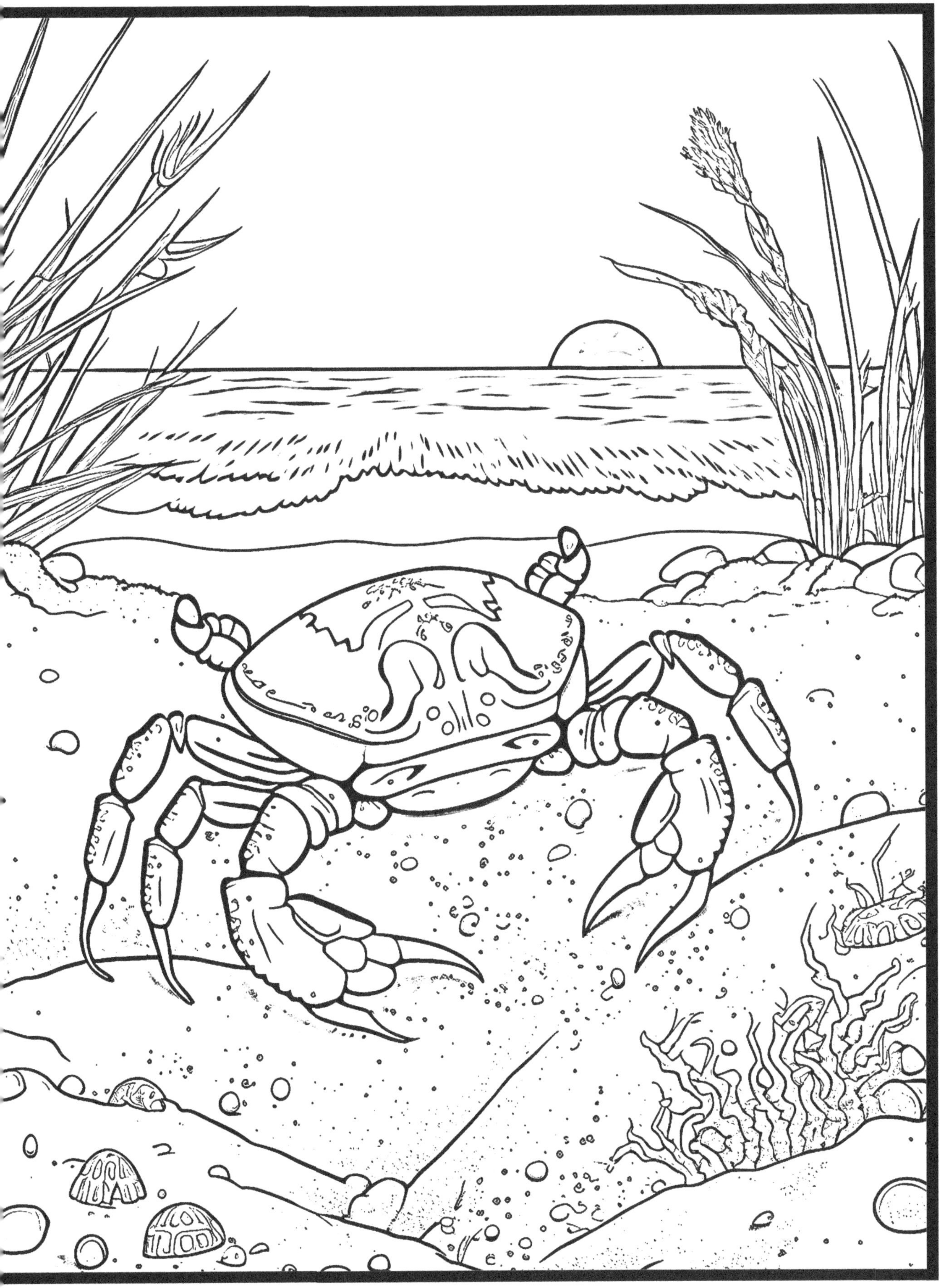

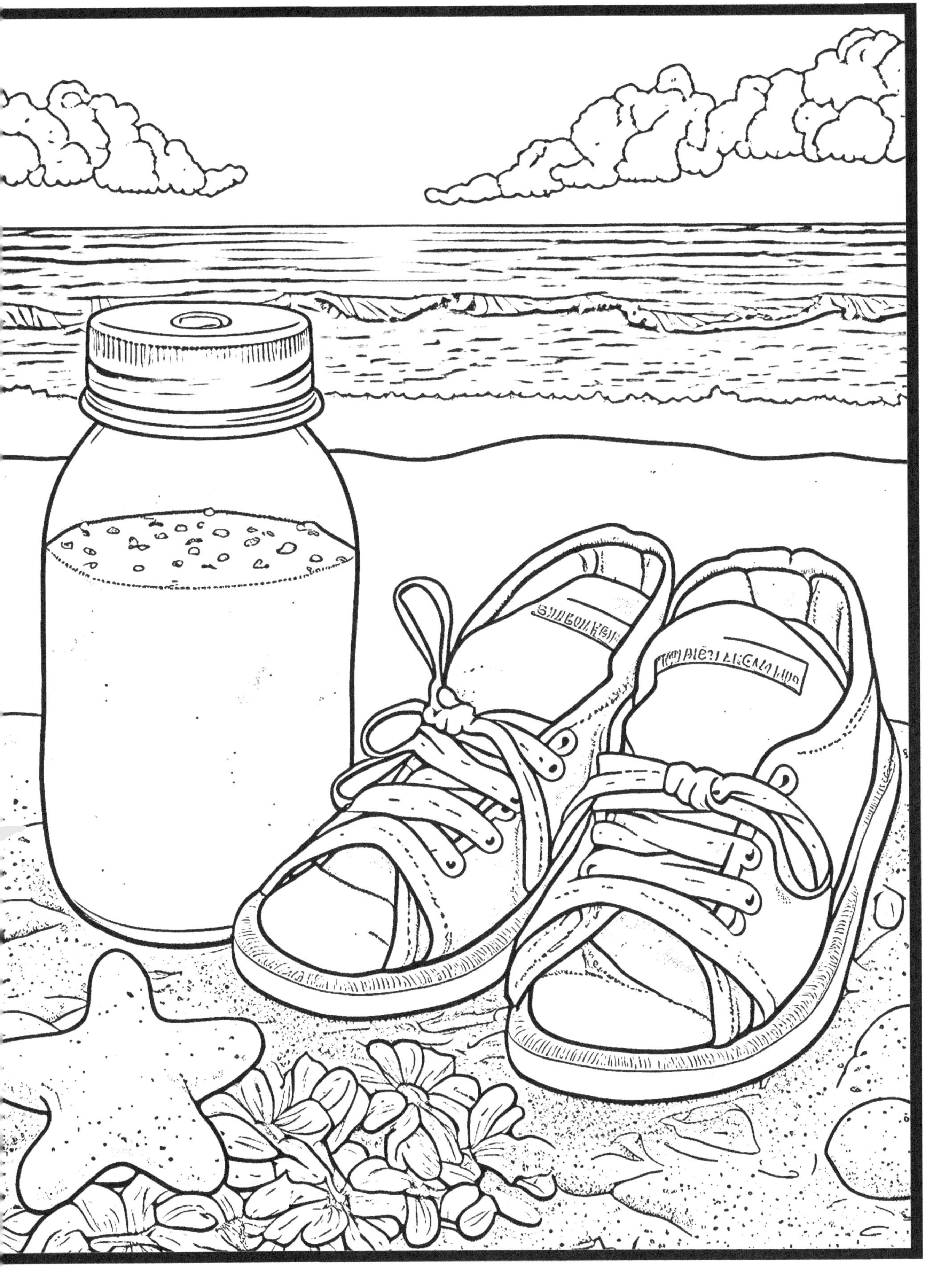

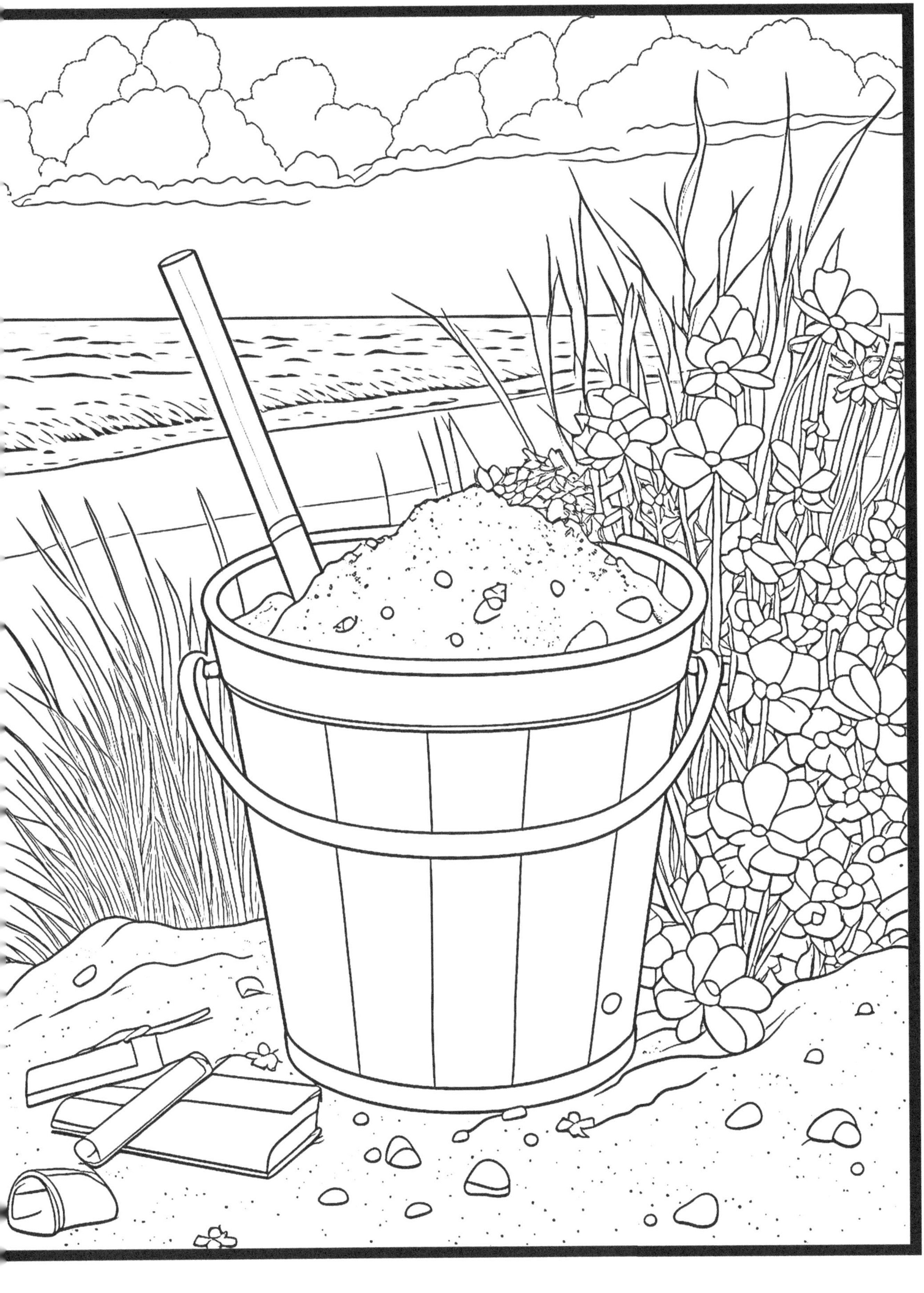

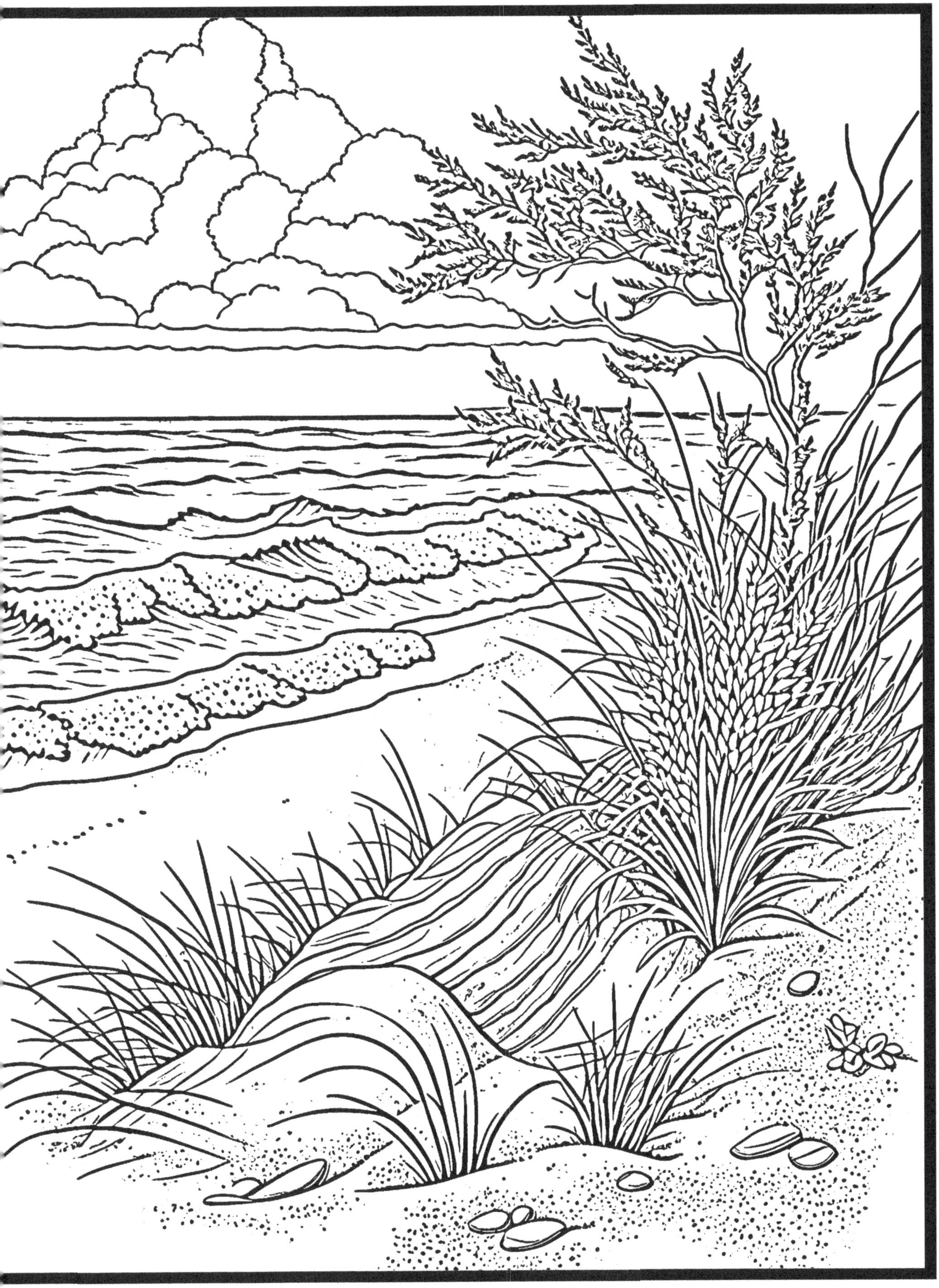

Made in the USA
Columbia, SC
25 July 2024

39325588R00057